THE BREASTFEEDING GUIDE FOR THE WORKING WOMAN

Also available from Century

The Breastfeeding Book *Maire Messenger*
Exercises for Childbirth *Barbara Dale & Johanna Roeber*
Postnatal Exercises *Barbara Whiteford & Margie Polden*
Toddler Taming *Dr Christopher Green*
Twins *Averil Clegg & Anne Woollett*

THE Breastfeeding Guide FOR THE WORKING WOMAN

ANNE PRICE & NANCY BAMFORD
FOREWORD BY LYNN REDGRAVE

SELECTED FOR THE BOOK LIST OF LA LECHE LEAGUE
OF GREAT BRITAIN

CENTURY PUBLISHING
LONDON

Anne Price and Nancy Bamford have both been La Leche League certified leaders and teachers in the United States. The publishers would like to thank La Leche League of Great Britain for their assistance in adapting the book for the UK.

First published in Great Britain in 1984
by Century Publishing Co. Ltd,
Portland House,
12–13 Greek Street, London W1V 5LE

British Library Cataloguing in Publication Data

Price, Anne
The breastfeeding guide for the working woman.
1. Breast feeding 2. Women—Employment
I. Title II. Bamford, Nancy
649'.3 RJ216

ISBN 0 7126 0413 8
ISBN 0 7126 0414 6 Pbk

Illustrations by Kenneth Reseigh Waters

Filmset by Deltatype, Ellesmere Port
Printed in Great Britain in 1984 by
Butler & Tanner ltd., Frome, Somerset

Acknowledgements

WE GRATEFULLY ACKNOWLEDGE:
Marion Galant for her kind donation of public relations and editing skills, but mostly for her belief in our endeavour and her ever-confident support.

Chele Marmet, Kittie Frantz and Jo Ann Touchton for all the work they have done to help women breastfeed, and for lending their knowledge and support to us.

Dr Usha Varma for her initial suggestion that a book like this needed to be written, and that we were the people to do it.

Our beautiful models—Debra, Maren and Brin Schwartz; Nancy and Catie Rullo; Geri and Noah David; Connie and Ian Ellefson; Janet Erickson; Ellen Prommersberger; Jill and Jamie Roth; Lev Price; Shira Salzberg; David Richman, Linda and Aylana Siegel-Richman; Shell, Lisa, Stephanie and Kacie Cook; Marion and Ariel Galant; and the students in Nancy Rullo's dancing class.

Our families—Neal, Lev, Mikki and Gabriel Price; and John, Tad and Tucker Bamford for their belief in us and their love, support and encouragement from the moment of conception through the labour and birth of this project.

The many other people who have offered help, information, advice and support, such as all the women who related their personal experiences and answered our questionnaire. We can't possibly thank them all individually here, but we do hope that they will accept our thanks for their important collective contribution to this effort to help other women.

Foreword

When my third baby, Annabel, was about six months old, my husband and I took her, as we often did, to a party. When she woke during the evening, I sat in our host's bedroom breastfeeding her. Soon one of the guests came in. "Do you mind if I watch?" she asked. "I've never seen a woman breastfeed a baby before." This woman had two children, but she said it had never occurred to her to breastfeed them, and no one had suggested it, either.

Living as we do, in a time when the extended family is often scattered, when most of this generation's mothers were bottlefed, the new mother looks around in vain for help and guidance and examples of breastfeeding as a simple, natural part of bringing up her baby.

Breastfeeding provides more than the best food. It is more than the most convenient method. It is the beginning of the language of love. Through this special bond with the mother, the baby first learns to receive love and in doing so grows to be a person who can love in return.

When my first child was born fifteen years ago, I breastfed him not without some problems. How I wish I'd had this book then. I knew nothing of the growth spurts that made him need to feed more frequently. When these happened, I assumed I didn't have enough milk, and instead of feeding him more often to build up the supply, I gave him a bottle. The vicious circle began. No one that I knew was breastfeeding, my doctor recommended supplementing with a bottle, and my mother had brought me up at a time when you breastfed at four-hour intervals and that was that. More might spoil the baby!

When he was five months old I had to do a film in Singapore. He was too young to have the required immunization shots and, fool that I was, I stopped breastfeeding and left him behind. Little did I know that had I kept breastfeeding him, he would have been protected by my immune system and could have come with me. The separation was ghastly for us both.

It's taken me many years and three babies to find out what my instincts could have told me from the start about breastfeeding and the bond it creates between mother and child. We've come a long way, baby, but civilization has dealt us a few rotten blows along the way. Gradually we are working our way back to nature.

A book like this is invaluable. More and more women are deciding to follow their instincts and breastfeed their babies. More and more new mothers return to work refusing to give up the special closeness and comfort that breastfeeding gives them and their newborn babies.

Yes, unfortunately women everywhere are still being forced to choose between their jobs and their children— but every time a woman succeeds in combining breastfeeding with a work situation, it sets a precedent. Employers see that it need not pose a threat to them; on the contrary, the happy employee is a greater asset.

Recently I filmed a public service message, promoting breastfeeding in the maternity ward of my local hospital. As I held a newborn baby in my arms I said, "When our babies leave this hospital, they are going to need all the help they can get. Breastfeeding gives them the best we've got."

It does. And it gives us joy when we feel our babies' touch; and peace as they relax, sated in our arms; and wonder at the miracle of nature that has given us this gift.

Lynn Redgrave

Contents

Introduction

"ANNE, WHY DON'T you write a book on breastfeeding for the woman going back to work?" When my obstetrician, Dr Usha Varma, a new breastfeeding mother who had just returned to work, made that casual suggestion to me, I realized that there was indeed a great void in breastfeeding literature, especially in light of the increasing number of working mothers. I phoned Nancy and pointed out that between the two of us we must surely have the knowledge and resources to successfully complete such a project.

We have spent a collective fourteen years in close contact with large groups of breastfeeding women. During this time we have seen many women who, like Dr Varma, have decided for reasons of their own to go back to work after their babies were born. These women strongly desired to continue the breastfeeding relationship, but many were unable to find adequate information to successfully combine breastfeeding and working.

In order to supplement our experience, knowledge and resources, we interviewed experts and numerous women who have successfully combined these two parts of their lives. In addition to the insight gained from our research and interviews, we present basic breastfeeding information and some of our own mothering philosophy.

Our purpose in writing this book is simply to fill the void, to make it possible for you to continue breastfeeding if you return to work. We'll not advise you to work or not to work after your baby is born—there are many other books that do that. We will instead assume that you have made that decision and offer practical alternatives for carrying out the choices you have made.

The semantics of all this require a little note here. Face it, "working mum" is a pretty useless term. For an employed woman it is a put-down; "working" is merely the adjective, implying that "mum" is what she really is, and the job is incidental. For the full-time mother, it is condescending to imply that she doesn't work. (Every mother is a working mother, right?) However, as meaningless as it may be, as laden as it may be with poor connotations, it is the only term conveniently available to differentiate between the woman who is employed outside the home and the woman who is not. "Working mother" is simply the most practical terminology. So we'll use it—begrudgingly—and, worse yet, we'll lump several different types of women into that category. When we say "working mother", we are speaking to the woman who is employed outside the home full time (forty hours a week or more), to the woman who is employed outside the home part time, to the woman who is studying full or part time, to the woman who earns money in her own home, or to any woman who finds the occasion to use any of the information we are setting forth.

Another semantic problem we face is the issue of referring to "the baby". Since babies come in both hes and shes, we have simply alternated by chapter our arbitrary reference to the baby by sex. (We have also decided to refer to babyminders and childminders as "she", since most minders are, in fact, female. We do not mean to imply that male minders cannot be equally competent and loving.)

The use of the American word "formula" has been retained in this edition because in Britain we don't have a similarly concise expression for "cow's milk specially modified for consumption by human infants".

We hope this book will help you enjoy your breastfeeding experience and enjoy your baby.

1/Advantages and Benefits

WHY WOULD ANYONE want to breastfeed a baby *and* work? Good question! Although we present basically a how-to book, it is of no value unless the reader has a good reason to want to know "how to".

Women choose to breastfeed when they become aware of the advantages, which are so abundant that no one book could possibly cover them all. And there are many studies currently under way that will undoubtedly bring to light new insights about the superiority of breastfeeding. We will discuss many of the major advantages, both as they apply to all mothers and also in relationship to the special circumstances and concerns of the employed mother. In addition, you will also discover others through your personal experience. Some may be more meaningful to you than the obvious ones.

HEALTH AND PHYSICAL DEVELOPMENT

The physical health of breastfed babies is better than that of bottlefed babies. This is a fact! Breastfed babies experience *seven times* fewer infections than their bottlefed counterparts. Of course, this is not to say that your particular breastfed baby will definitely be healthier than your neighbour's bottlefed baby, but when the two groups are compared statistically, breastfed babies are ill far less often.

There are several reasons for the lower rate of infection among breastfed babies. For one thing, a breastfed baby receives antibodies from his mother's colostrum and, later, from her milk. Colostrum is the premilk fluid that is present in a mother's breasts in late pregnancy and the first days postpartum. It is a thick yellow liquid designed specifically for an infant's early days, and it is higher in protein and calories than breast milk. It helps clear mucus from the baby's throat, and its laxative effect helps clear out the stool that accumulates *in utero,* called meconium. Colostrum probably gets the most acclaim, though, for its immunological properties, and deservedly so. It provides babies with antibodies which protect them from disease. Recent research on this subject was published in the *Journal of Pediatrics*.[1] The authors report that this immunological protection does not diminish with time as was once believed. In fact, high levels persist throughout the first year of lactation, and the preliminary data indicates that these levels are maintained throughout the second lactating year as well.

In addition, for as long as the baby is ingesting nothing but breast milk, that milk creates an acidic environment in the baby's intestines, one which discourages bacterial growth.

Many authorities also feel that when a baby drinks a bottle on his back, the pressure resulting from his sucking can cause some milk to enter his middle ear. This can lead to an ear infection. However, a breastfeeding mother does not have this concern. "Sucking" at the breast does not create the same type of pressure as "sucking" a bottle, nor is the baby flat on his back while feeding.

The most obvious advantage of breast milk is that it is nutritionally perfect. Human milk has evolved over millions of years to become the perfect food for the development of human babies. Milk designed for another species simply cannot compare.

The balance of the various ingredients of breast milk is geared towards brain growth, rather than large muscle growth, as is cow's milk. For a fascinating breakdown of the various components of breast milk and their roles, read Chapter 10 in La Leche League's *The Womanly Art of Breastfeeding*.[2]

If you are breastfeeding, you can rest assured that your baby will be as healthy as he can possibly be and that he will reach his genetic potential in size, intelligence and beauty. This is quite an insurance policy!

Fewer breastfed babies are allergic, and again there are several reasons, one being that colostrum performs a task called "gut closure". When a baby is born his large intestines are somewhat permeable and whole proteins (from food or formula) can pass undigested through the intestinal walls. His body then produces antibodies to the substance,

[1]Goldman, Garza, Nichols, and Goldblum, "Immunologic Factors in Human Milk During the First Year of Lactation", *Journal of Pediatrics* C #4 (April 1982): 563–567.

[2]La Leche League International, *The Womanly Art of Breastfeeding* (La Leche League International, 1981): 281–304.

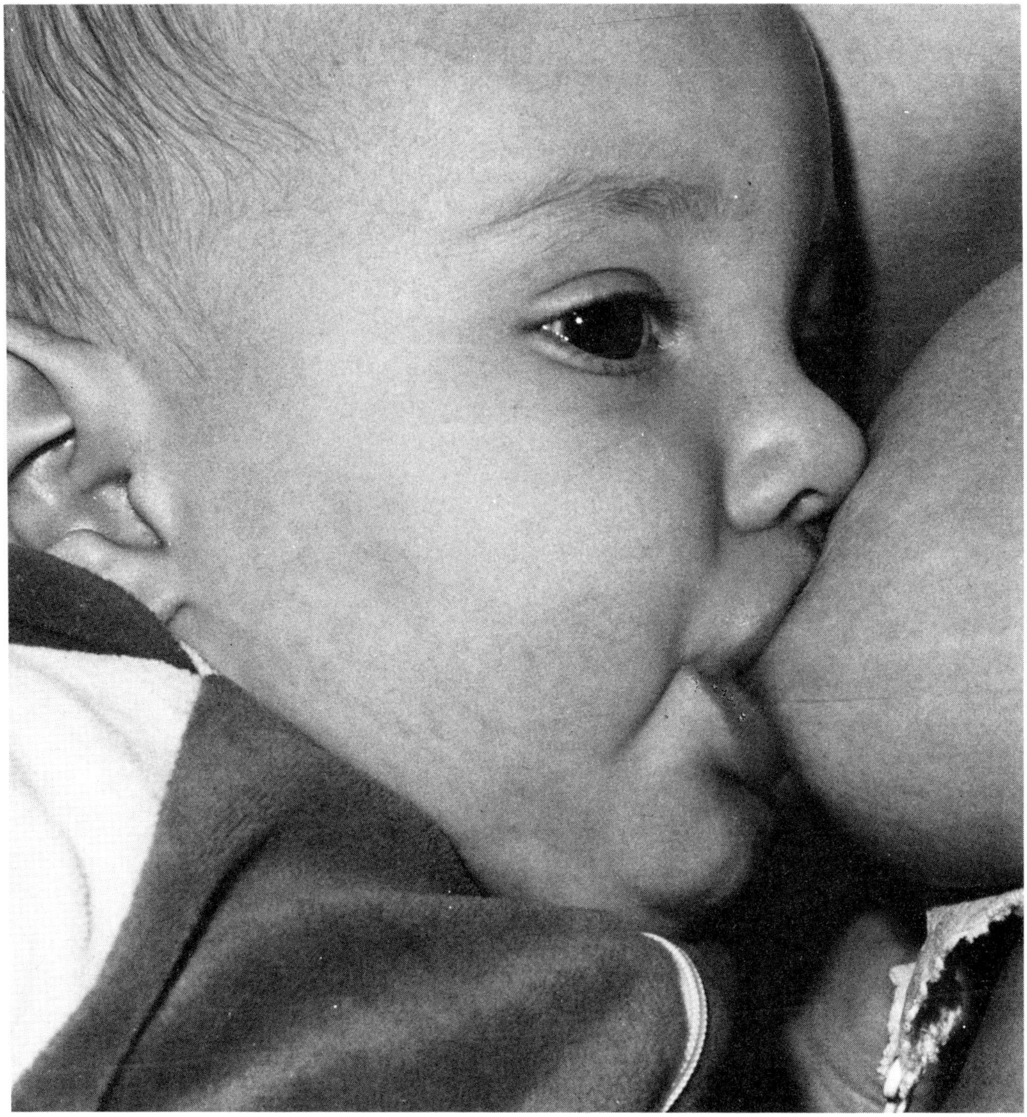

A breastfed baby usually has a healthy glow to his skin and a general look of well-being. (Photo by Harvey Schwartz)

thus developing an allergy. However, when a baby ingests colostrum, the intestinal permeability is so greatly decreased that those whole proteins remain within the intestines to be properly digested and no allergy results.

Breastfeeding also prevents allergies because breastfed babies avoid exposure to cow's milk, which is an extremely common allergen at an early age (under twelve months). Other foods can also cause allergic reactions if introduced at too early an age. Since breastfed babies generally begin eating solids at a later age than their formula-fed counterparts, they have less chance of developing that type of allergy.

In a paper presented at the La Leche League International Convention in 1964, Dr E. Robbins Kimball presented the following dramatic correlations from a study of 1,378 children:[3]

		ALLERGIC BABIES	
Number of Babies	*Duration of Breastfeeding*	*With Family History of Allergy*	*Without Family History of Allergy*
268	0–4 days	7.5% (20)	4.1% (11)
136	less than 1 month	7.4% (10)	2.9% (4)
123	1–2 months	7.3% (9)	2.4% (3)
323	2–6 months	5.3% (17)	1.2% (4)
528	6 months plus	4.0% (21)	0.0% (0)

At this point it is appropriate to mention that it is impossible for a baby to be allergic to his own mother's milk. It *is* possible for a very sensitive baby to react to something his mother ingests which goes through her milk. The most common offenders are dairy products, wind-producing vegetables such as broccoli and cauliflower, iron supplements, and large amounts of carbonated beverages, caffeine or nicotine. Remember that a food sensitivity is not an allergy. After all, each of us as adults react differently to different foods, too! Also bear in mind that a very sensitive baby is rare, and if your baby has times when he cries, it is unlikely that it is at all related to your diet.

Since breastfeeding was carefully designed by nature, it makes sense that it enhances almost every aspect of both the baby's and mother's

[3]Kimball, "Optimal Infant Nutrition", La Leche League International Convention, 1964 (La Leche League International Information Sheet No. 203): 5–6.

lives. The simple act of breastfeeding has numerous advantages. For one thing, it helps the shape of the baby's mouth to develop properly. When a baby sucks on a bottle, his mouth must conform to the teat. With breastfeeding, however, the mouldable flesh of the nipple conforms to the baby's mouth, allowing it to develop naturally.

In addition, the development of the jaw is enhanced. When a baby feeds at the breast, he must use a vigorous pumping action with his jaw. This action causes his jaw to develop to its genetic potential and contributes to the facial beauty of the child.

A stronger, more developed jaw will also be an asset in other areas. For instance, breastfed babies are more likely to have straight teeth and need a brace less often than bottlefed babies. The proper shaping of the mouth and jaw are important factors in the alignment of the teeth. Also for these reasons, there is a tendency for speech to develop more clearly in breastfed babies. This is not to say that breastfed babies never need speech therapy, but it will be necessary much less often.

These are just a few of the abundant physical advantages a breastfed baby receives. Breastfeeding is a lifetime investment in health, and a gift so easily given to your baby.

EMOTIONAL AND PSYCHOLOGICAL DEVELOPMENT

Although the physical benefits of breastfeeding are truly impressive, they are probably surpassed by the emotional plusses. The importance of bonding or attachment cannot be overemphasized. The bonding process is one that makes you feel overwhelmingly attached to and "in love with" your baby. The future of your relationship with your child depends greatly on the quality of the bond you form with him during infancy.

Two main elements in bonding, eye contact and physical closeness, are provided for in a perfect way by breastfeeding. The early feeds, which may seem superfluous because of the small amount of nourishment the baby actually takes from the breast, serve the purpose of providing for each of these two elements.

The newborn is biologically geared to look for the human face and can focus best (even on a moving object) at about ten to fifteen inches. And not so amazingly, when a baby is at the breast, that is usually the distance from his eyes to his mother's face. As you feed, your baby will probably stare at your face intently, and you will undoubtedly gaze back

Love glistens in the eyes of this baby as she returns her mother's adoring gaze.
(Photo by Harvey Schwartz)

in love and amazement. This is much like young lovers—they can stare into each other's eyes for hours!

The second element in the bonding process is physical contact. As you hold your infant close to your body in the breastfeeding position, you can't avoid skin-to-skin contact, and you will find yourself instinctively stroking and touching him all over. Since a new baby feeds frequently, this supplies the large amounts of close-contact time you both need.

Of course, no one would suggest that a bottlefeeding mother will not bond to her baby; what we are saying is that successful bonding is hard to avoid when you breastfeed your baby.

In addition to the initial attachment process, the wonderful skin-to-skin contact and frequent times of closeness which a breastfeeding pair experience go a long way towards establishing emotional security and happiness for your baby. The continuity provided by the breast-feeding relationship is another factor in building the security we all hope our children will have.

You will hear people say that breastfed babies are more spoiled or demanding than other babies. Although there may be an element of truth in that, it's stated incorrectly. Very often, breastfeeding mothers are so tuned in and responsive to their babies' needs that they unknowingly communicate, "You can trust me. I believe your needs are legitimate and you can make them known to me and count on me to satisfy them." This is exactly what a baby needs to learn in order to establish real trust in his parents (and later in the outside world) and develop true emotional security. So when a breastfed baby seems more spoiled and demanding, it is usually a sign that the baby feels loved enough to express his needs.

BENEFITS TO THE MOTHER

Even if you are not impressed by all the wonderful physical and emotional benefits associated with breastfeeding, the convenience alone is certainly something worthy of acclaim. Almost every breast-feeding mother, when asked about the aspects of breastfeeding she values most, will rank ease and convenience at or near the top of her list.

Granted, bottlefeeding need not be as much bother as it used to be. Formulas are easier to mix or can be bought ready to use. But some chores simply cannot be eliminated; it's still necessary to buy bottles and formula, take them from refrigerator to travel bag to car to the shops and back, and of course wash and sterilize them. Can you imagine finding that bottle you lost last Saturday with one ounce of curdled milk left in it?

For the breastfeeding mother, all of that bottle-carrying and washing is eliminated. As long as you know how to breastfeed (read about it *before* your baby is born) and have no major complications (like a baby who is ill), the only work to breastfeeding is pulling up your shirt and putting baby to breast. In fact, when we hear a mother say, "Oh, I don't want to go to all the bother of breastfeeding", we can't help but wonder, "What? All the bother of pulling up your shirt?"

Of course, this great convenience is diminished when a mother works and begins carrying bottles to the babyminder daily. But for that mother, during the hours she doesn't work the conveniences are even more greatly appreciated! The fact that she does not need to prepare or heat formula when she is at home (especially at night) saves a great deal of time, a precious commodity to any working mother.

Breastfeeding also saves a significant amount of money. This is an advantage even to the mother who pumps breast milk, as the one-time expense of a breast pump and bottles can be considerably less than that for months of buying baby milk powder. At the time of this writing it costs approximately £1 per day to formula-feed a baby. That comes to almost £150 for a six-month period. Breastfeeding is, of course, free.

You may have heard that it is necessary to eat more when you are breastfeeding, so you will be spending more on your own food. This is true only if you are a very thin person and you are concerned about the gradual, natural weight-loss which occurs during breastfeeding. Most women, however, are delighted to lose the weight; they simply eat to satisfy their hunger and make no effort to consume extra calories.

No one will argue with the fact that early motherhood can be very trying. But here again, nature's plan is evident. When a woman is breastfeeding, her dominant hormones are prolactin and oxytocin (as opposed to oestrogen and progesterone). Each of these hormones serves us in a unique way. Prolactin is sometimes called "the mothering hormone". It has the effect of causing extremely maternal feelings to ooze through your system, which serve to make you uneasy when you are away from your baby. And doesn't it seem natural that your feelings of needing your baby should reflect the intensity of his need of you?

Because you will feel closer to your baby with prolactin in your system, you may wonder whether it is wise to continue breastfeeding after you return to work. Let us assure you that the effect will still be a positive one. You will miss your baby while you are at work—you may

A breastfeeding break is both relaxing and satisfying to mother and baby alike.
(Photo by Harvey Schwartz)

hold on to him all the more when you are with him—but you will surely adjust to your new lifestyle. In fact, many feel that this very close attachment is especially healthy for a working mother and her baby because it gives an extra and exclusive intimacy to their relationship.

The hormone oxytocin is called "nature's tranquillizer", and it lives up to that name. At one time or another most breastfeeding women have observed that regardless of how harassed they may feel, once they settle down and begin to breastfeed, a wonderful relaxing sensation comes over them. This is the effect of oxytocin. During this demanding and trying period of our lives (our years of nurturing babies and toddlers), doesn't it seem only fair that we have a continually refillable prescription for a free, natural tranquillizer?

In addition to these pleasant feelings which have a biochemical source, many women also report a psychological sense of well-being. Somehow the idea of living out one's "feminine life cycle" is very satisfying. As women, we know there are many special things about our bodies. Giving birth is certainly a peak experience. Breastfeeding, too, is a natural and wonderful gift which is uniquely ours to give.

The physical health of the mother is enhanced in many ways as a result of breastfeeding. When a baby sucks, oxytocin is released in the mother's system; this, in turn, triggers uterine contractions. If you breastfeed on the delivery table, it will help to expel the placenta. The contractions you have in the weeks following delivery are also very beneficial to your uterus. They help prevent haemorrhage and help return your uterus to its original pre-pregnancy size and shape. Because of this, some hospitals will allow mothers to be discharged only hours after they give birth, but only if they are breastfeeding.

Another benefit which is greatly appreciated by breastfeeding mothers is the delay of menstrual periods. A nonlactating woman has a dominance of the hormones oestrogen and progesterone in her system, and they regulate her normal menstrual cycle. When lactating, frequent nipple stimulation maintains a dominance of prolactin and oxytocin, and the decrease of oestrogen and progesterone brings about the suppression of her regular cycle. Any prolonged decrease in breastfeeding, such as occurs when the baby starts eating solids or sleeping through the night, or when the mother begins a full-time job, could bring about a change in the hormonal picture which could then reinstate the menstrual cycle. So you should be able to count on not having a period during the time you are breastfeeding exclusively. Many women do not have a menstrual period for a year, even after the baby begins eating solids, and occasionally a woman may even go two years without menstruating.

Of course, the reproductive system is delicately balanced, and every woman is different. The possibility mentioned above is not a prediction of what will or will not happen for any particular woman.

There are several reasons for you to be happy about this absence of menstruation (called "lactation amenorrhea"). The first is simply the convenience and welcome absence from possible period pains. In addition, you do not run the risk of anaemia and fatigue from the blood loss connected with your periods. There is also a decreased possibility of pregnancy. Generally, the first one or two periods are without ovulation. Although you cannot absolutely count on it, chances are slim that you will become pregnant without having had a period first. Remember, however, that lack of periods cannot be counted on as a sole, reliable method of birth control.

Some authorities believe that having fewer periods can also decrease your chances of developing cervical cancer. According to this theory, a woman is not meant to have one period after another during all of her childbearing years. She is meant, biologically, to have breaks from menstruation. Think of a woman in a totally "natural" state—let's say the cave woman. Shortly after her first period she probably would have conceived, then breastfed for at least two years, then conceived again, etc. Most of her childbearing years would have been punctuated with three-year breaks from her periods.

Now look at the modern woman. She probably has two nine-month breaks from menstruation during her lifetime. Perhaps the hormonal environment of her cervix during these many menstruating years could be a contributing factor to the occurrence of cervical cancer in modern women.

On the subject of cancer and breastfeeding, we should also refer to the relationship between breast cancer and breastfeeding. Although authorities do not feel that breastfeeding is the only factor related to reduced breast cancer, it seems to be one of them. M. Levin and Associates did a study which linked the length of breastfeeding to protection from breast cancer.[4] According to the study, if you breastfeed for a cumulative period of seventeen months or more there is a decreased risk of breast cancer. Among women who have a breastfeeding history of thirty-six months or more there is a "marked decline" in the rate of breast cancer. This can mean breastfeeding one child for

[4]La Leche League International, *The Womanly Art of Breastfeeding* (La Leche League International, 1981): 320.

thirty-six months or six babies for six months each. At any rate, although the evidence is still inconclusive, there seems to be a correlation between breastfeeding and a lower incidence of breast cancer.

Many women find that one of the most appreciated side-effects of breastfeeding is the weight loss which generally accompanies it. During pregnancy, your body stores calcium, fat and nutrients which you will need during lactation. If you breastfeed, your baby uses up these stored supplies. Consequently, you lose weight. It is estimated that you use between five hundred and a thousand calories a day breastfeeding, depending on the age of your baby and how much milk he is taking. One thing to be aware of, however, is that this weight loss is slow and gradual, not an overnight process. Many women will despair after two or three months because they have not lost all the weight they want to lose. It takes time. The longer you breastfeed, the more you will lose.

Some women find that they lose a large amount of weight immediately after birth and then experience a slow but steady loss. Others have a weight-loss pattern of sudden drops and plateaux. If you are not losing as quickly as you had hoped and it is a source of anxiety for you, you can speed things up by staying away from desserts and snacks. Don't forget, though, that your appetite will probably be very good and your energy needs high, so be sensible about weight loss. You have the rest of your life to be thin, but only this short time to be a source of nourishment to your baby.

So why bother with breastfeeding? Because breastfed babies are physically healthier in many ways. Because breastfed babies have an extra opportunity for optimal emotional and psychological development. Because breastfeeding saves time, saves work and saves money. And because a breastfeeding mother gains many extra health and emotional benefits.

FROM A WORKING MOTHER'S POINT OF VIEW

Do these advantages hold for the working mother? Does their significance fade or gain new importance? How do these advantages relate to the working mother? We must admit, in all fairness, that a working/breastfeeding mother does not really reap all the advantages a full-time breastfeeding mother does. However, many of the rewards she experiences will carry far greater significance in light of her particularly demanding life. There can be no question that she and her baby receive many advantages they would miss if they were not a breastfeeding couple.

A working mother is by definition an overloaded person. She needs every convenience possible to make her lifestyle more viable and any saving in time or work is valuable to her. Any working person knows how it feels to arrive home from work too tired to move. But unless you've been there, you can't appreciate the psychological difference between being able to sit down immediately to the relaxation of feeding your baby and having to face the ordeal of preparing a bottle while jiggling a tired, impatient baby on your hip.

Certainly, the inconvenience of expressing breast milk cannot be discounted. But when you are at home, breastfeeding without worrying about the preparation of bottles makes life easier and leaves more time for other activities.

The fact that breastfed babies will be healthier is probably one of the most crucial benefits to a working mother. Obviously each of us wants a healthy baby for the baby's sake. But a healthy baby also makes Mum's life far easier, both by simplifying her day-to-day physical activities and by easing the emotional pressures on her.

It is a very serious problem for a working mother to have a sickly baby. In addition to dealing with the normal parental anxiety for the well-being of the baby, someone is usually required to miss work, as the babyminder will probably not want to look after a baby who is ill. Of course, it may be possible to alternate days at home with your partner, but most families discover that when he's ill, a baby often wants only his mother. So, theory aside, it is usually the mother's problem when the baby is ill. At night, too, when a baby who's ill is up more often, he usually prefers Mum.

A healthy baby also contributes to your peace of mind. Apart from the extra work for you and discomfort for your baby, the real concern and anxiety that go with an infant's illness are an extra drain in themselves. You'll either be at work worrying about your baby or at home worrying about your work!

The fact that you, as a working/breastfeeding mother, know you are giving your baby the best physically, nutritionally and emotionally has to reduce your stress and anxiety level. In her book *Nursing Your Baby*, Karen Pryor offers encouragement to mothers who are working and breastfeeding: ". . . when the baby is nine or ten months old or older, it is almost easier to work or finish studying if the baby is breastfeeding than if he is not. The closeness of the breastfeeding relationship, the

The breastfeeding relationship sets in motion a cycle of love that quite naturally extends to include the whole family. (Photo by Anne Price)

reassurance of the breast when you come home each day, make your absences easier for the baby to tolerate and makes him a cheerier, less demanding baby when you come home.

"No matter what the baby's age, the mother who works and breastfeeds should really be proud of herself. She is working extra hard and doing the best she can do for her child."[5]

Besides making your life easier, the benefits of breastfeeding will magnify the happiness in your home. The closeness and the continuity you put into your relationship with your baby will build a firm foundation of love and security. A happy baby is easier to love. This sets up a wonderful cycle—your lovable baby gets more love and attention and thus becomes even more sociable, alert and irresistible.

By the same token, a less harassed mother is also more loving and lovable. The time and energy saved by breastfeeding will also contribute to your good spirits. Feeling secure about your baby's well-being and sharing a very special relationship with him will enhance your positive feelings about motherhood and life. All of this is sure to improve not only your relationship with your baby but the one with your partner as well.

The extended skin-to-skin contact you and your baby experience is a very special element in your relationship. You can suggest that your partner partake of this sensory joy of parenthood, too. Bathing the baby is the perfect way for the father to have skin-to-skin contact with his baby. Once the baby is a little older, showering together can be fun, too. Cuddling and rocking are always open to Dad. And having the baby sleep with you is an easy way for the whole family to experience a physical closeness which has effects that last well into the day. Although some families may not be comfortable sleeping with their baby for fear of hurting him, we do not feel there is any danger and there is no evidence to dispute our beliefs.

DISPELLING SOME MYTHS

What about some of the "disadvantages" to breastfeeding you've heard about? The most common point cited to discourage women from breastfeeding is that it will tie them down. In the case of a working woman who is skilled at pumping and storing her milk or plans to leave formula, this cannot apply. During your off-work hours, breastfeeding

[5]Pryor, *Nursing Your Baby* (Pocket Books, 1973): 234.

may tie you to your baby more than bottlefeeding would, but this is certainly a plus for your baby and his emotional development.

Will breastfeeding ruin the shape of your breasts? No. Pregnancy will cause your breasts to enlarge and perhaps even develop stretch marks, but this happens regardless of whether you breastfeed or not; it is simply a side effect of pregnancy. Actually, it is believed that not breastfeeding—not using your breasts for their intended biological function—will cause them to atrophy sooner. At the end of each breastfeeding relationship your breasts will feel very empty and flabby, but about six months after you've stopped feeding they should resume their approximate pre-pregnancy shape and size.

You may have heard that your diet will be very restricted. This is just not so. For example, you need not avoid spicy foods unless your baby has an unusually sensitive stomach. If yours is one of those rare babies, try looking at foods like cabbage, excess sugar, carbonated beverages, excess caffeine or other foods to which you react. Cut down on smoking. Of all the women we have counselled, we have encountered only *one* whose baby reacted negatively to chocolate!

Of course, you do need to be careful about ingesting drugs. Actually, most medicines are safe for a breastfeeding mother to take, but always check with your doctor first. For instance, one drug which presents a real problem to breastfeeding mothers is the birth control pill, even the "mini-pill". You absolutely cannot take birth control pills if you breastfeed. They will diminish your milk supply and the hormones will get into your milk. However, there are so many other methods of birth control available that this should not present a major problem to any one.

By now you may be convinced that breastfeeding is the superior way to feed a baby. These many benefits count extra for the working mother. You can reassure yourself that it is well worth the effort for you, your baby and your partner to continue your breastfeeding relationship after you return to work.

2/Getting Off to a Good Start

HOW THE BREAST WORKS

Before we can discuss how breast milk gets into the baby, you need a clear picture in your mind of how the breast works. The internal structure of the breast can be compared to a river system with the tributaries merging as they travel. These are called lactiferous ducts. Deep within the breast, at the beginning of each of the tributaries, is a grapelike cluster of milk-producing cells called alveoli. On this site the

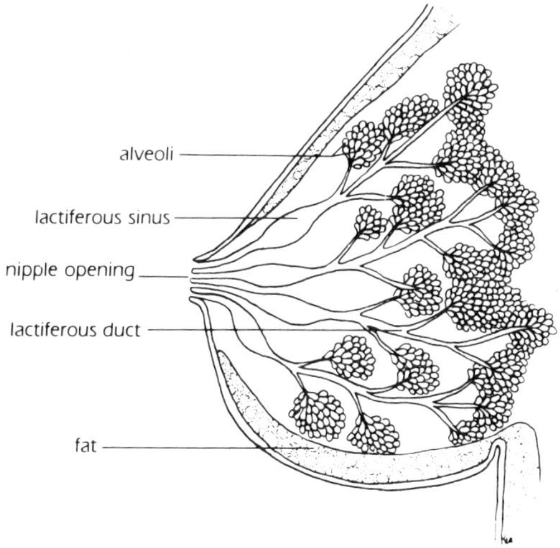

Anatomy of the Breast

ingredients which will go into the milk are extracted from the bloodstream and the milk is produced. Surrounding the alveoli are threadlike arms which form a netlike cell. When the baby sucks, and thus stimulates the nerve in the nipple, a message is sent to the pituitary gland in the brain. It signals the release of two hormones: prolactin, which causes the milk to be secreted, and oxytocin, which causes it to move through the ducts. So, as a direct result of the baby's sucking, this "net" snaps down and literally squeezes the milk into the lactiferous ducts leading to the nipple. The milk then travels downwards in the duct to a reservoir called the lactiferous sinus, which is just behind the darker skin surrounding the nipple, called the areola. This is called "the let-down reflex".

When this reflex occurs many women feel a tingling or a mild ache. Although it may sound uncomfortable to a woman who has not breastfed, most mothers find the let-down sensation to be quite pleasant in that it evokes very motherly and nurturing feelings. However, in the early days of a breastfeeding relationship, most women have no sensation of the let-down, and as the baby grows out of infancy, some women lose the sensation again. It is important to separate the sensation from the function: it is relatively rare for a woman not to *have* a let-down, but it is not at all rare for a woman not to *feel* a let-down. On the other hand, if the let-down reflex is very strong, some milk may leak out or even spray out of the nipple openings.

How does the baby get milk out of the breast? Through the process we just described, the stimulation of the let-down reflex causes the milk to come down to the nipple. However, the baby must also do her part. The baby takes the nipple into her mouth and draws it backwards with an upward and pulling motion by her tongue. She holds it in place in the back of her mouth with negative pressure and then begins a pumping motion with her jaws.

BASIC HOW-TO

Hopefully you will want to educate yourself thoroughly by reading other books on breastfeeding. Although there is a great deal more that can be said on the subject, we would like to discuss some of the most basic aspects of how to breastfeed.

The first step you need to take to achieve successful breastfeeding is nipple preparation. The simple procedure that we outline can greatly reduce your chances of experiencing sore nipples after the baby is born.

During the last few months of pregnancy, you should do "nipple pulls" a couple of times a day. To do these, you simply lubricate your nipples and areola with lotion or lanolin, and then pull and twist them several times. (Do this firmly but gently—it's not supposed to hurt.) As a result, you will have nipples that are pliable and elastic, *not* nipples that are tough. Nipple soreness from early feeds results from the nipple being stretched far back into the baby's mouth. It is easy to see, then, that toughness enhances the chance for soreness, but elasticity certainly decreases that possibility.

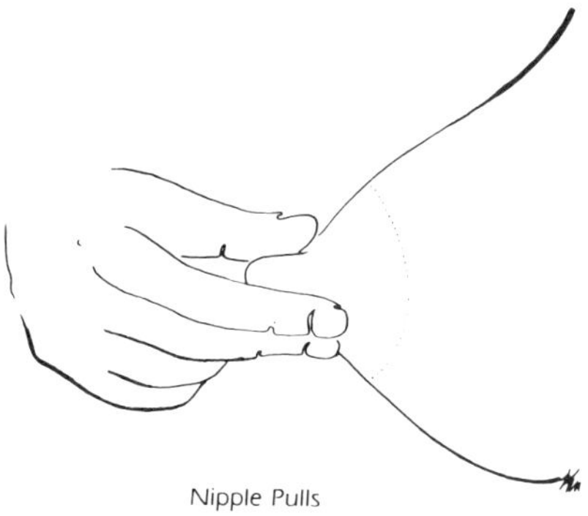

Nipple Pulls

Once your baby is breastfeeding, there are additional measures which you can take to prevent soreness. When you have finished a feed, air-dry your nipples, and always try to keep them as dry as possible. *Never* put a bra on with wet nipples, and *never* wear a bra that is wet. After the nipples are dry, some women apply a thin coat of a moisturizer like pure lanolin, available without a prescription at many chemists. (If you are allergic to wool, you will be allergic to lanolin, too, since it comes from sheep's wool. Also avoid lotions with perfumes and alcohol, since they will be more irritating than soothing.) You only need to do this in the early weeks. Remember to wipe off the excess before feeding, so that the baby does not ingest it.

It is also very helpful to frequently alternate breastfeeding positions. Sit up for one feed and lie down for the next. Lying down to feed may feel awkward until you discover the most comfortable position, but it can be wonderfully relaxing once you learn to do it. Changing positions changes the points of stress on the nipple, thus decreasing the chance of soreness. You may need to persevere in finding comfortable positions which take into account your height, body type and furniture.

Some doctors or nurses recommend that you feed for only one minute at a time on each breast the first day, two minutes the second day and three the third. They feel that this will help to prevent sore nipples, but actually all it will prevent is adequate nourishment for the baby. It takes longer than that to have a let-down in the beginning, so this type of restrictive feeding is not beneficial to mother or baby. In general, there is no need to worry greatly about limiting the time of feeding, even in the beginning. The length of time you feed is really not the cause of sore nipples. If you get sore nipples with unlimited breastfeeding you probably would have got them anyway a few days later with limited feeding. Should you get sore nipples despite preventive measures, see the section on treatment in Chapter 5.

Positioning the baby properly is most important to breastfeeding efficiently and avoiding sore nipples. La Leche League, an international organization which provides information and encouragement to breastfeeding mothers, has much to offer in this area. We know of a mother, Jan, who fed her first baby for about two months, during which time the baby gained very little weight. She said, "I also had sore nipples during the entire time I breastfed Dana. After hearing the correct breastfeeding position described at a La Leche League meeting, I discovered what the problem had been.". Jan's baby had been feeding not on the areola, but on her nipples alone with the baby's mouth open very little. Dana had been unable to get any great quantities of milk from her mother's breasts, since she was not pumping the lactiferous sinuses. She was probably only receiving the milk which came out with the let-down reflex. This milk is high in nutrients and protein but since it is low in fat, she gained very little weight. In addition, Jan's sore nipples were unavoidable because the pressure was exerted directly on them.

Kittie Frantz, a qualified nurse, has developed guidelines for getting the baby on the breast correctly. Ms Frantz is the director of the Breastfeeding Infant Clinic at the Los Angeles County University of Southern California Medical Center and has been a La Leche League Leader since 1964. Her information is crucial to successful breastfeeding—make sure you understand each step.

Step 1: Place the side (not back) of the baby's head in the crook of your arm as you settle in to feed. Bring the arm which is holding the baby around her back and hold on to her top thigh or buttocks, with your palm facing towards you. You need to hold the baby securely in order to be able to control her position, then pull her bottom towards you. Make sure the baby's whole body is facing yours so that you are face to breast, abdomen to abdomen, knees to belly, etc.

Step 2: Hold your breast with your now-free hand. Place *all* the fingers under the breast and the thumb on top of the breast, behind the areola. This position allows you to support your breast for the entire feed, if necessary. Sometimes this is needed with a tiny infant, especially if you have large breasts. If she has to use all her strength to hold your breast in her mouth, she won't have much left for good sucking. This position of your hand also keeps your fingers behind the areola, so they won't interfere with the area the baby needs to take into her mouth. (This is the disadvantage of the more common "scissors hold".) Holding the breast this way also allows you to move your nipple up and down and to centre it in the baby's mouth. If you push in with your thumb, your nipple will point up. If you push in with your fingers, it will point down. Try it—it works! Pointing the nipple downwards often makes it easier for the baby to take the breast properly.

Step 3: Bring the baby up to the breast and tickle her upper lip gently with your nipple. Within a few moments, this should cause her to open her mouth wide. Do keep it gentle: your baby won't respond to mashing your nipple against her lips. When it is open very wide, centre your nipple, then pull the baby close. Don't pull her close if her mouth is not open wide, or if the nipple is not in the centre. Wait until everything is right. When she is feeding properly, her bottom lip needs to be curled out. You may read elsewhere that your entire areola must be in the baby's mouth, but this is not always possible or necessary. Some women simply have a larger areola than others, so it is impossible to state definitively how much areola will go into the baby's mouth. Your nipple will reach to the back of her mouth when she is feeding properly, which means that at least a great deal of your areola goes into her mouth.

If you follow this procedure, chances are very good that your baby will suck with great efficiency, and that you will not have sore nipples. If it doesn't hurt, then you can be fairly certain that the baby has the breast in her mouth properly and your position is good. It may sound as if you are going to great lengths to engineer something which should be natural, but in fact you are simply overseeing the natural process. Very quickly this all becomes habit, so it is wise to establish good habits from the very start. If you feel you need to see further diagrams of this positioning, you can contact La Leche League for their reprint No. 11, "Managing Nipple Problems", by Kittie Frantz, RNCPNP. Reprints are available at any League meeting or from La Leche League of Great Britain, BM3424, London WC1V 6XX.

Even though you have successfully positioned your baby on the breast and she is feeding well, it would not be uncommon for you to wonder if you have enough milk for her. Some mothers even go so far as

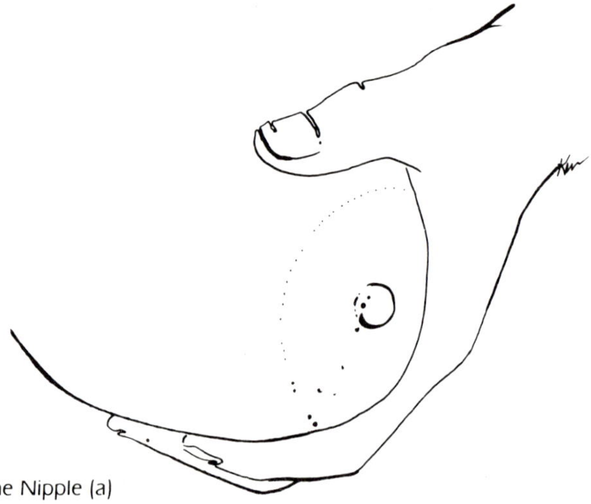

Centering the Nipple (a)

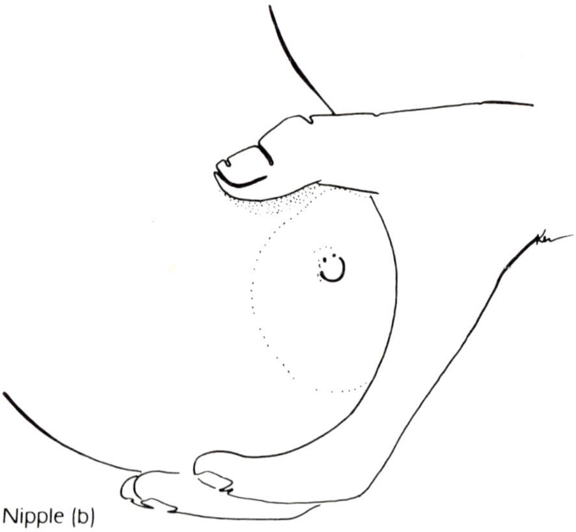

Centering the Nipple (b)

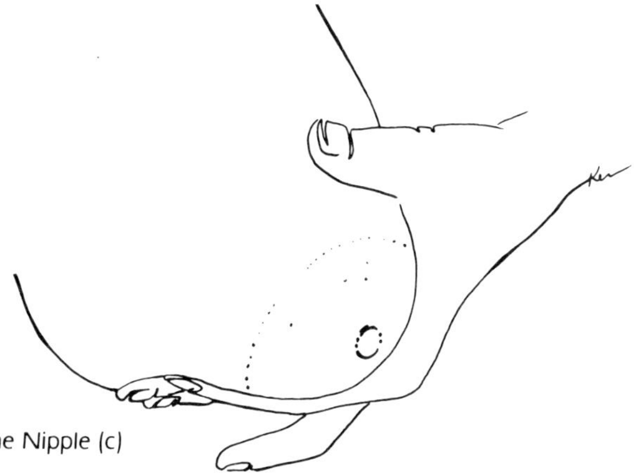

Centering the Nipple (c)

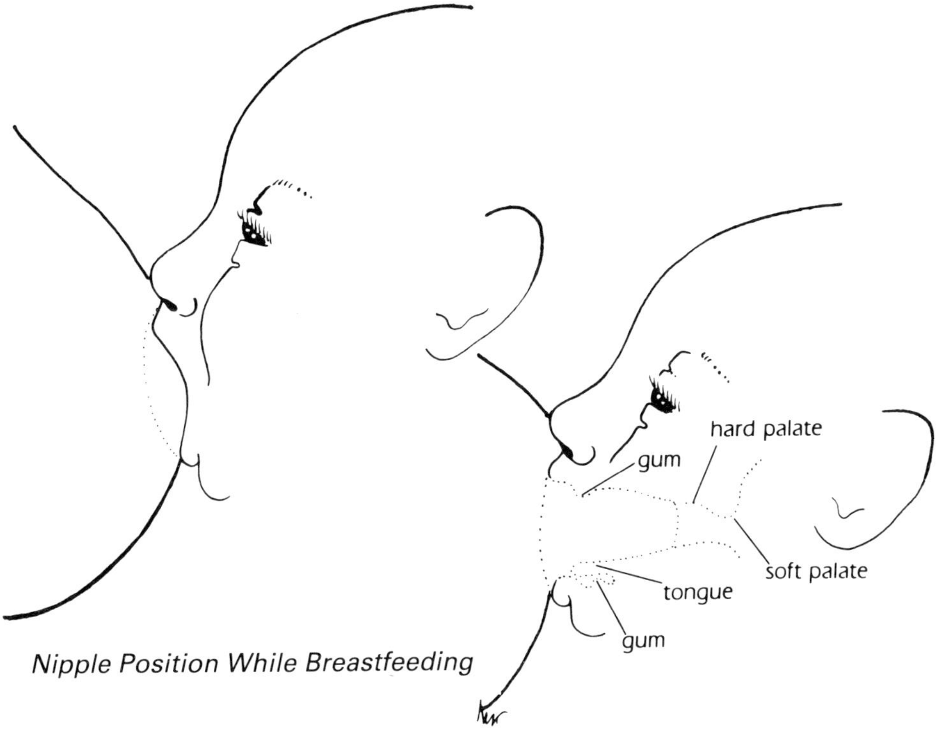

Nipple Position While Breastfeeding

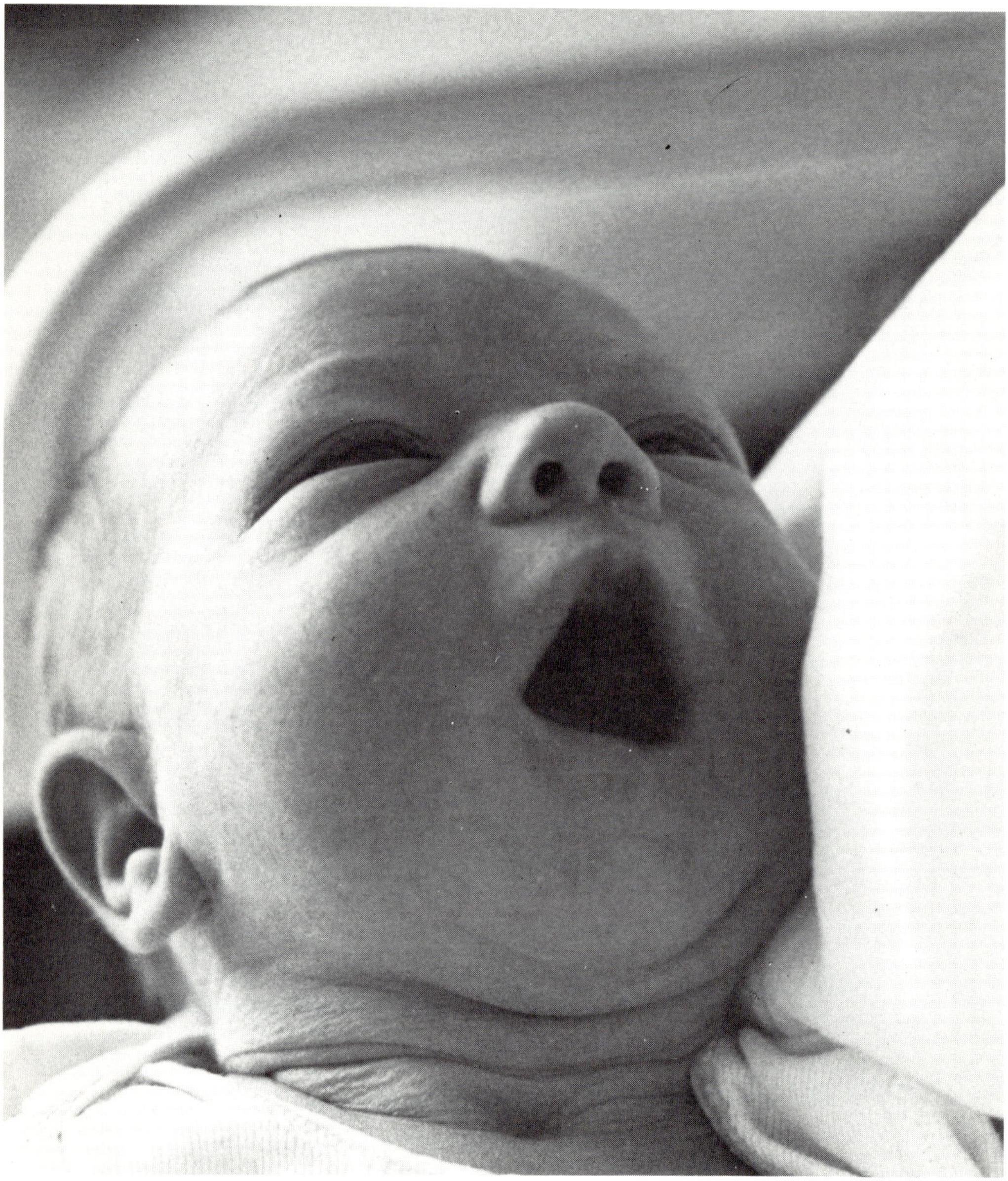

This hungry baby has his mouth open wide; he's ready to feed even before his mother is. (Photo by Neal Price)

to "test weigh", that is to weigh the baby before and after each feed! Although it may be reassuring, it is certainly unnecessary. With rare exceptions, if breastfeeding is being managed correctly, there should always be the right amount of milk for your individual baby.

In the early days after your baby is born you will produce colostrum, a very valuable substance for your baby. Within a few days your milk will "come in". You will probably have more milk than your baby needs at that point. In these early days you may feel engorged or over full and have some leakage. This is due to the supply-and-demand nature of lactation; up to this point your body has had no demand to which it can regulate the supply.

The milk-making mechanism can be compared to a computer. The baby "programmes" it by taking out the amount of milk she needs. By doing this she relieves a certain amount of pressure from within the breast. It is believed that the breast takes its information on milk production from this pressure. In other words, the less milk that is emptied, the less milk the breast is programmed to produce. The more often and more thoroughly the breast is emptied, the more milk the breast will produce. For this reason, it is important to try to get the baby to feed on both sides each time. Both sides need stimulation and emptying to keep production up. Occasionally, however, there are babies who insist on feeding on just one side each time. These babies seem to empty that one side more thoroughly, and generally they do well. It is still better, though, if you can get your baby accustomed to feeding on both sides each time.

One aspect of breast milk we will mention here is the variation in fat and nutrient content. The milk the baby gets in the beginning of a feed is called "foremilk". This milk, which comprises about one-third of a feeding, is thin and watery with little fat and few calories. It does, however, contain many nutrients. The milk the baby gets at the end of a feed is called "hindmilk". This milk has a high percentage of fat and a high calorie content, although not many nutrients. Obviously, it is essential that the baby gets both the foremilk and the hindmilk in order to grow properly. This is another reason to allow her plenty of time at the breast.

An old misconception which one will occasionally still hear is that, to increase her milk supply, a mother must "save" it and feed less often. This mistaken notion has caused many women to diminish their milk supply, ultimately to the point at which they are completely unable to nourish their babies.

If your baby experiences a growth spurt (often occurring a few days after birth, six weeks, three months and six months), she may need more milk than she has been taking. The clear remedy is to feed more often, so that the baby's hunger will be satisfied and she will "reprogramme the computer" at the same time. She will feed very frequently, perhaps every hour or two (or in some cases even more often), for a couple of days. This will increase your milk supply and then she can gradually go back to her normal pattern. A common cycle seen, and one to avoid, is one that does not allow the baby to "reprogramme the computer" to greater quantity. In this frustrating scenario, the mother feeds the baby a formula supplement when the baby requires more than she can supply. Then the baby has less desire to suck at the breast because she is less hungry, which results in less milk, more supplement and so on. It's better by far to work through a few taxing days of extra breastfeeding and build up an adequate supply again the natural way.

How often should you feed your baby? Letting your baby set her own pattern is the best idea, since only she knows when she is hungry. This is called "demand feeding". However, there are some rather placid new babies who go more than four hours between feeds or sleep through the night. It is not a good idea to let new babies go more than three or four hours between feeds, and they should feed at least once during the night for about six weeks. (This time period is very approximate, because there is great variety in babies' birth weight, weight gain patterns, and their eating and sleeping styles and needs. Many babies don't sleep through the night until they are much older still, so don't hesitate to go to your baby when she cries in the night, no matter how old she is.) Most new babies will feed approximately every two or three hours around the clock. These times will probably get farther apart as the baby gets older.

We are often asked how soon after a feed there will be enough milk for the baby to feed again. You can feed a baby as often as you (and the baby) want to. Your breasts are continually producing milk. If you feel your milk supply is down, feed more and you will build it up. Although it probably takes about two hours before your supply is completely replenished, don't feel you have to wait that long to feed again, because there will always be something there. If you are working and pumping instead of breastfeeding during much of the day, you will find it necessary to keep up night feeds and frequent weekend or day-off feeds to keep up your supply. If you can view night feeds with this in mind, they may seem more like a blessing than a nuisance. Many women find that they need a minimum of four feeds in a twenty-four-hour period, on the days they work, to maintain an adequate supply. These are usually in addition to the pumping they do at work.

IN THE HOSPITAL

Good beginnings are crucial to a successful combination of working and breastfeeding. Since birth is clearly the beginning of your breastfeeding relationship with your baby, it is the time to get off to a good start. Of course, giving birth is a giant topic in itself; we'll just consider it briefly in relation to breastfeeding.

The choices in our society in the area of birth are many. It is your responsibility to choose a safe, appropriate place for your baby's birth. It is your responsibility to provide your baby (*in utero*) with optimal prenatal care, such as premium nutrition, avoidance of drugs and adequate rest and exercise. And it is your responsibility to educate yourself to the greatest extent possible about pregnancy, nutrition, childbirth, breastfeeding and being a parent. Only an educated consumer can fully enjoy the responsibilities we've laid out. So read,* take all the classes you can find and discuss it all carefully with your partner.

As you become more educated and gain a greater understanding of your needs, you can begin to lay the groundwork for birth. Communication is vital in this stage. Your partner must know your needs to begin to help you meet them; your medical attendant and the hospital staff, too, must know your needs in order to deal effectively with them. Discuss with your medical attendant the type of birth you want, the procedures that you want or want to avoid, and the amount of involvement or lack of involvement you desire from your loved ones and the hospital staff or midwife if your baby will be born at home. Know in advance what the hospital policies are, and when you are admitted let the hospital staff know what *your* policies are!

And finally, lay the groundwork for your homecoming. Arrange for some help—your mate, mother, mother-in-law, a sister, a friend or hired help. Most of us find that this is a period worthy of selfishness on the new mother's part. *Do* pick someone who will support your mothering and breastfeeding, who will cook and clean and shop for you, who will grant you peace to mother and breastfeed and rest. Others can come later as guests, but in the beginning you need help.

*See the booklist on p. 98 for helpful books on birth.

Hopefully, by the time you get to the hospital you will be well prepared, but there are also some specific things you can do in the hospital to greatly enhance the start of your breastfeeding relationship. Many hospitals have instituted family-centred maternity care, in which the family unit is separated much less than usual. We support this method enthusiastically and feel that it greatly enhances a peaceful, unstressful start for the new family. Consider taking advantage of this policy if your hospital follows it.

The first few hours with your new baby are vital to bonding as a family. The most important thing to do in the early hours is to take time to fall in love with your new baby. Touch, admire, kiss, examine and generally feel free to get close. Don't worry about the careful hospital "gift wrapping" they give your baby—getting close is what's important.

All babies are very different, so be prepared to be flexible. Some seem to be born with the knack for breastfeeding and will latch on and suck easily right away. Some will have a great desire to suck, but not be able to work out how to do it. Others will merely nuzzle or lick at the breast and some seem too sleepy to even try.

Keep in mind that breastfeeding stimulates hormones to expel your placenta and contract your uterus to its pre-pregnancy size, so it is very healthy to breastfeed at this time. Even nuzzling can stimulate this hormonal release. But equally important is that grand skin-to-skin contact and discovering the feel and scent of each other! Enjoy and extend every moment together immediately following birth.

Two little problems that seem big in the first hours with your baby are how to get the baby on the breast and how to get the baby off the breast. Feeding is an art to be learned and sometimes simple aspects like these loom large when we are faced with them for the first time. Familiarize yourself with the procedure for getting the baby on the breast which we outlined in the "Basic How-to" section (p. 18) before you go to the hospital, and you'll decrease the anxiety of first feeds. Getting the baby off the breast is a simpler matter. Just break suction by inserting your finger in the corner of her mouth.

The remainder of your hospital stay differs from the first few hours in many ways. Once you are settled in your room, feeding becomes nourishing as well as nurturing. This is the time to position the baby properly in order to start good habits. This is the time to begin demand feeding, which means feeding the baby whenever she cries or otherwise indicates that she wants to feed. Let the baby set her own feeding pattern unless she goes more than four hours between feeds.

You and your baby are probably both better off if you notify the

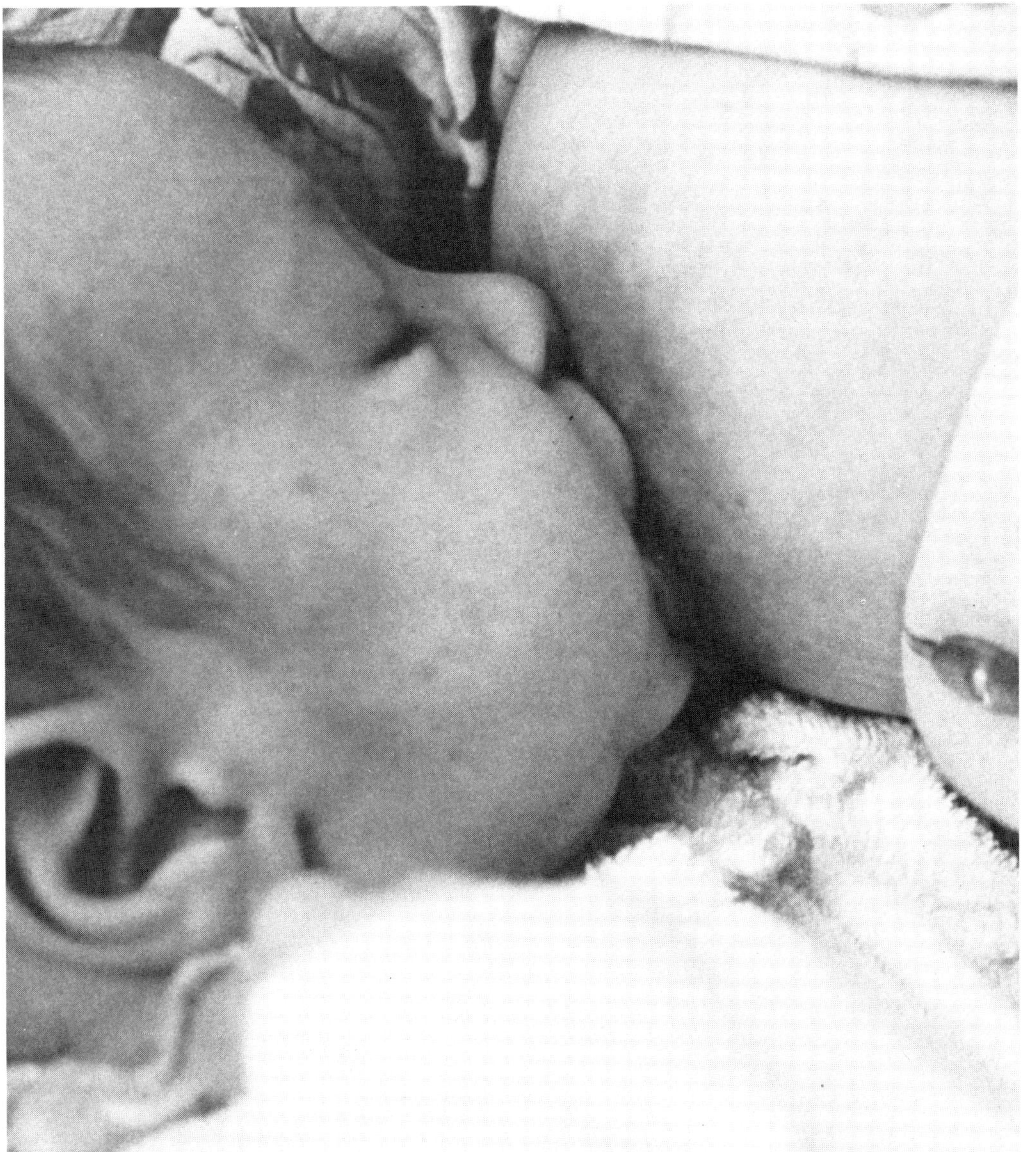

Increased confidence in your mothering abilities can come from trusting your baby and following her cues. (Photo by the University of Colorado Health Science Center)

hospital staff not to give any formula or glucose water to your baby. Supplementing is a common practice, but for a healthy baby who is demand fed, there is no need for it. Also, supplementing will partially satisfy your baby's hunger and sucking desire, so she will suck less at the breast. Why start fooling around with the supply-and-demand system before it has a chance to work? And why give the baby formula, when breastfeeding is available and healthier by far for mother and baby? Why let a nurse feed your baby when you have waited nine months to love and care for her?

This is the time for being together with your baby twenty-four hours a day. We heartily recommend this for two reasons. First, by allowing true demand feeding, it is better for your milk supply, better for your baby and better for your recovery. Second, it is ideal to begin caring for your baby while there are knowledgeable people around from whom you can receive help if you need it. We are sure your baby would rather have you dress her awkwardly than a nurse dress her neatly. Many mothers who allow the hospital staff to care for their babies feel overwhelmed by the necessity to furnish that care when they first arrive home. During the time at the hospital, involve yourself totally in your baby and her care and you will feel much more confident when you take her home. Finally rest, rest, rest—as much as possible. Some women like to stay at the hospital several days just to rest. Some find that the hospital is miserable and noisy and uncomfortable and not the least bit restful. So by all means, take your pick—home or hospital—but for the first several days do *nothing* but mother and rest.

Your early days at home should be an extension of the days at the hospital. You will feel better sooner if you do the Kegel exercises (see *Pregnancy and Childbirth* by S. Kitzinger) you may have learned in childbirth classes, and feed your baby often. Sleep when she sleeps, day or night. Let the housework go—your health is more important now.

Try your best to make this time at home with your baby peaceful and restful for both of you. We've heard a couple of ideas that work well in the early weeks at home. One is to have an attractive but comfortable dressing-gown to wear all day every day. This reminds your friends, family and yourself that this is a period for rest and recuperation, and yet you will look and feel attractive. No one will expect you to serve coffee and cake in your dressing-gown. Another idea along these lines is a nice wraparound skirt. Again this allows you to look and feel attractive and comfortable during the transitional phase between your maternity and regular clothes. As soon as you go back to work, there will never again be enough hours in any day, so take advantage of the

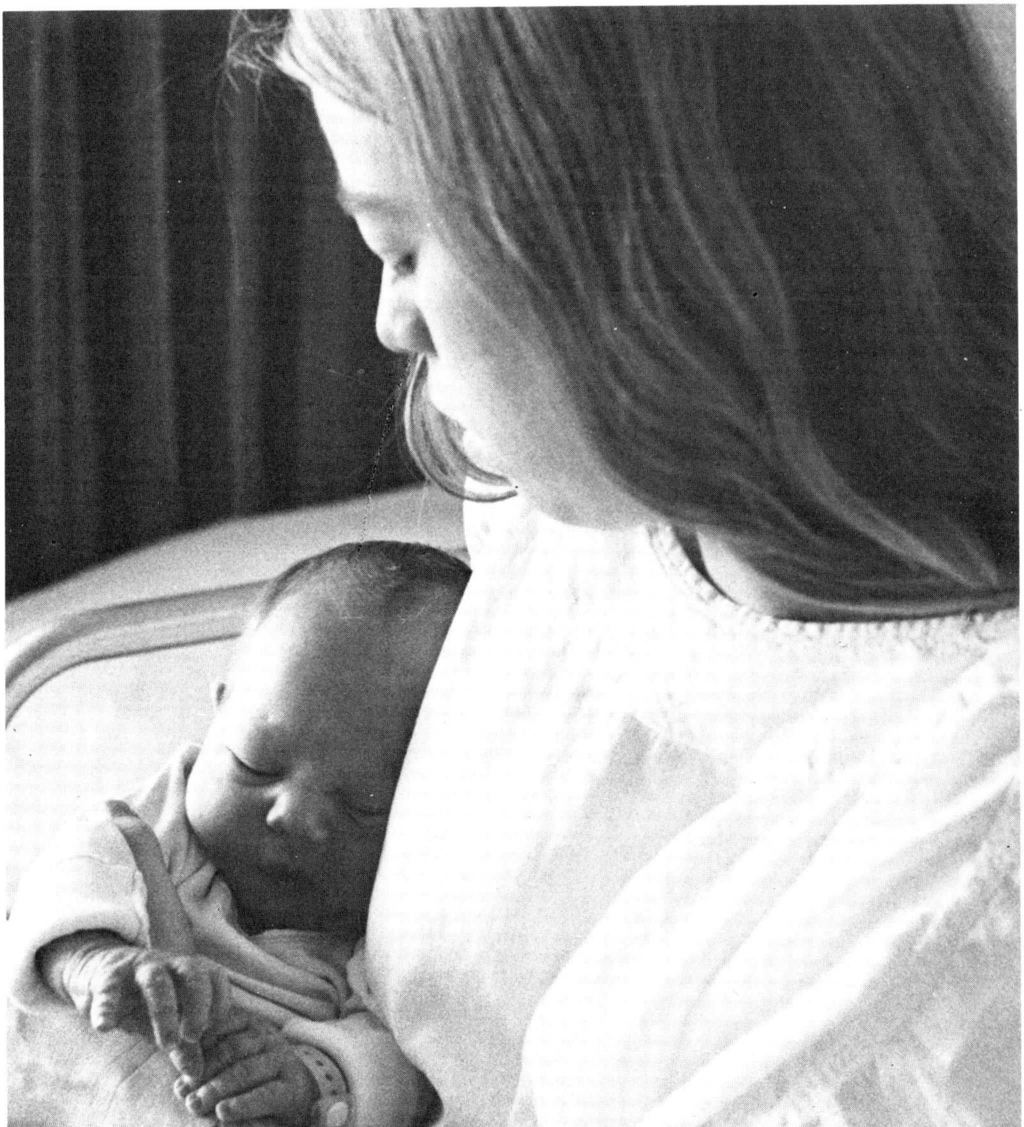

A new mother often feels awkward in her efforts to care for her baby. Yet there is a wonderful, magical quality in these early days which always seems to prevail over the normal frustrations of new motherhood. (Photo by Neal Price)

opportunity to rest and fully recuperate. Rest enough and you will greatly reduce the possibility of encountering depression ("baby blues") or illness.

Although we have discussed the normal birth experience, we realize that a certain number of you will have had Caesarean births. This will not affect your ability to breastfeed. You can begin to breastfeed in the recovery room and feed on demand from that point on. The pain medication you receive will not pass through your milk significantly. Take it, by all means, and breastfeed normally. Decreased pain will allow you to be more mobile, which will speed your recovery and will also make it more comfortable to handle and care for your baby. Your recovery will be only slightly slower than that of a woman who has had a normal delivery. You may need to delay having your baby by you twenty-four hours a day until the second or even third day, depending on how you feel.

Your birth experience, hospital stay and early time at home can range from harassed to rewarding. There is so much stress already inherent in the birth of a baby that you should strive to alleviate as much as possible. You may imagine that there will be lots of time to take care of things after the baby has arrived and before you go back to work, but we haven't yet met a woman who found that to be true. So do your preparation and education now. We can't say it too often: good beginnings are crucial!

3/Preparing to Go Back to Work

The time between the birth of your baby and the day you go back to work is a very important period. First and foremost, it gives you a chance to have some extended pleasant time with your baby. You will be getting to know each other and forming a close attachment or bonding. However, it is also the time during which you must lay the groundwork for successfully combining working and breastfeeding. There are several areas where you will need to make decisions, preparations and arrangements.

SELECTING A CHILDMINDER

Usually, the subject of greatest concern at this point is selecting a caretaker for your baby. The first question is, who will it be? This depends to a great extent on your work timetable. If your work hours and your partner's are different, or if he has taken paternity leave, he is probably the ideal person, because he shares your intense love for the baby. Some men are uncomfortable in this role and may resent it and the degree to which it ties them down. In this case, it may not work out. Sometimes it is possible for the father to do some of the caretaking, necessitating only a part-time childminder.

Some women have a mother or mother-in-law who is available and willing to care for the baby. This has both good and bad points. On one hand, his grandmother surely loves your baby more than a childminder would, and your child would probably be the only one being cared for in the home. If you feel good about your mother's or mother-in-law's mothering style and you have a good relationship with lots of communication, this may be a most loving choice. On the other hand, the grandmother may feel she can be a little more aggressive with her own childbearing ideas than someone you have hired. If there are going to be conflicts about how your child will be cared for (fed, put to bed, disciplined, etc.), you are less likely to "win" with the grandmother as caretaker.

A day nursery is another possibility, although not all of them accept babies. A few day nurseries are run by the state and are free. Others are private and you will have to pay. To find out what's available and how much it costs, contact your local social services department or health visitor. To find your health visitor *before* the baby's birth, seek her out through your GP's surgery. If you are interested in this option and know of a day nursery that takes infants, you will want to look into it carefully. Go—more than once—and observe. How many children are there? How many babies? What is the adult-to-infant ratio? How much time do the babies spend in cots? How much time being held, comforted or played with? How long are they allowed to cry? What is the turnover rate of the employees? Remember, they usually get paid very poorly. Talk to other mothers who use the facility. If you are truly satisfied with what you see and hear and with your own gut-level feelings, this may be a viable option for you.

Another possibility is to have a childminder come to your home or employ a nanny. This is the most expensive of the alternatives available to you. If you can afford this and feel that you would like to keep your baby in his own familiar surroundings, you can put an ad in the newspaper and start interviewing. Something you must realize, however, is that even though you feel as though you are spending a large sum of money for a minder, that sum, when seen as income, is usually very small. You are probably not going to find someone with impressive qualifications who will want to work for very little money.

Having the baby cared for in the childminder's home is probably the most common solution to the baby-care problem. As with the other options, this one has its advantages and disadvantages. In this case, though, the advantages usually predominate. The simple fact that a childminder in her own home can earn enough money to make it worth her while is usually a clue that she is very capable. Once again, however, it may be a little difficult to find a childminder who takes infants, but you should be able to find a few to compare. You can try to find childminders through your local social services department or your health visitor. A personal recommendation is better still.

A woman who minds children in her home will probably be reliable. Being a childminder is generally her business, and she works for more than one person. She is in her own home, which is most convenient for her. She is also not likely to give up suddenly. A childminder must be registered, and that means that her home has been inspected for safety. She may only mind three children under the age of five, including her own. (The childminder doesn't have to be registered if she is a close relative of the child, for example, the child's aunt or grandmother.)

When you visit your prospective childminder, you will want to ask about and look for certain features which satisfy your own needs. Many women have special concerns, such as maintaining a kosher or vegetarian diet, a particular religious environment or an unusual timetable. In addition, you will want to think about the following ideas.

Location is important. In general, it is better for you and the baby to find a minder close to work rather than close to home. This will mean less separation time and less wait to empty full breasts and feed an eager baby—not to mention less time at the minder's, therefore less expense. The time you travel together to the childminder can be a sweet time together. Instead of listening to the car radio, why not talk or sing to the baby? He may be the only person who will love your singing!

You should tell the childminder of your plans to breastfeed and observe her reaction. Hopefully it will be enthusiastic. If you plan to leave formula, the only special help you will need from her is cooperation. Ideally, the baby will be hungry and ready to feed when you arrive from work, but if he just won't wait, you want the minder to give him only a small amount of milk before you arrive to feed him.

If you plan to leave breast milk, you will definitely need the sitter's enthusiastic support. In addition to not feeding the baby too much just before you arrive, there is the element of the extra effort required for careful handling of breast milk. It will help if she herself has breastfed. She will appreciate the value of what you are doing and have some knowledge of it.

Also discuss your mothering style. You are paying her to be your substitute, not to "do her own thing". If you rock your baby to sleep rather than let him cry himself to sleep, tell her this. Share your feelings on eating. Do you prefer natural, unsweetened foods? Is it important that your child finish everything on his plate? Also discuss discipline. Do you want her to smack your child? Under what circumstances? Do you have certain approaches that you would like her to reinforce? Is she familiar with any current books that favour the philosophy you prefer?

Although many of these issues seem to relate more to the toddler or older child, they are still well worth discussing for two reasons. First of all, there is the chance that you will stay with the same childminder for several years and, secondly, the caretaker's philosophies tell you a great deal about the person to whom you may entrust the care of your child.

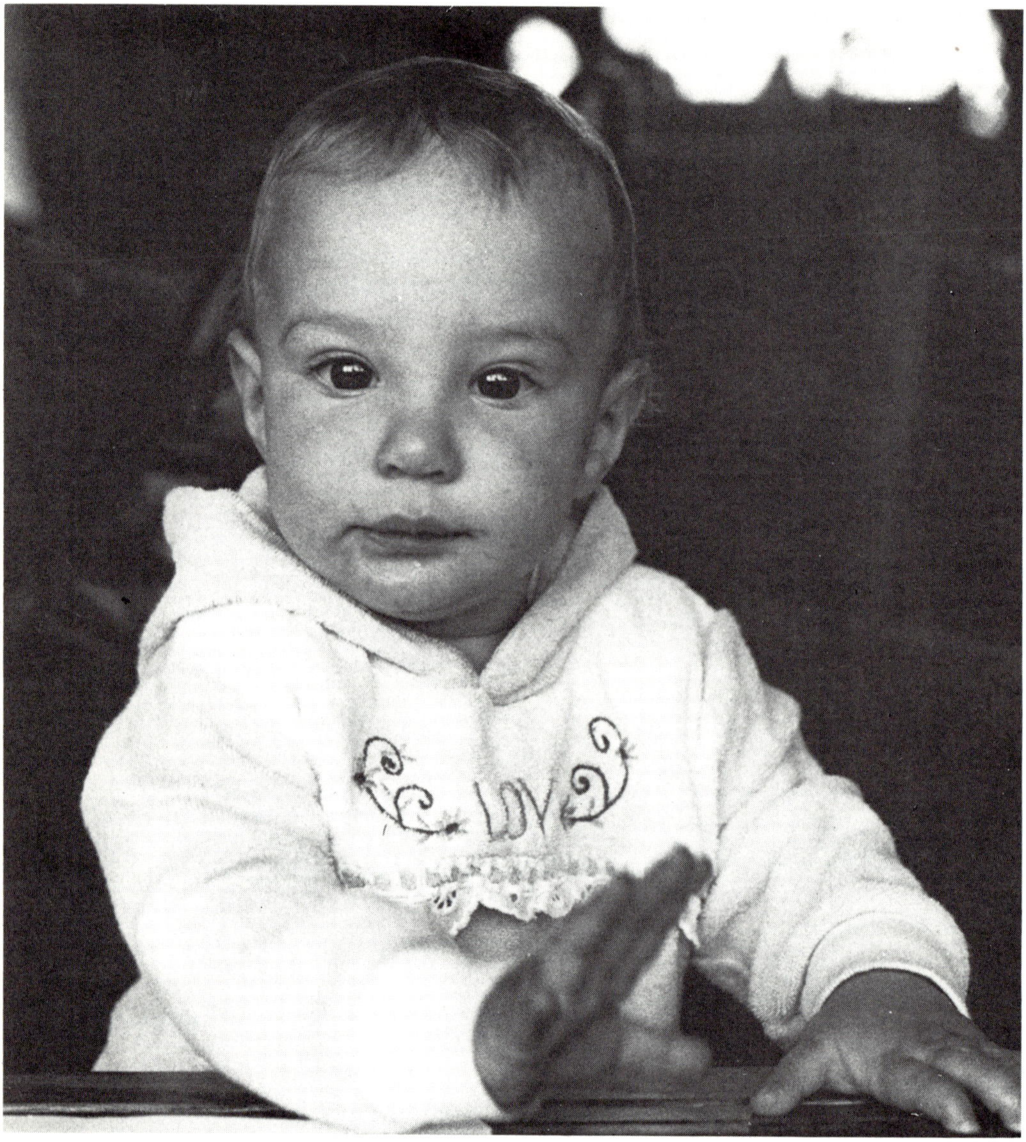

This baby looks impatient for her mum to arrive from work for the long-awaited five o'clock feed. (Photo by Harvey Schwartz)

Another way to help you assess the babyminder is to arrange your first meeting at around eleven-thirty a.m. or four-thirty to five p.m. These are likely to be the worst, most harassed times of her day so you will probably see her under stress. How is her patience? How does she deal with tired, crabby, hungry children? Does she seem to have the sort of calm nature needed for this type of work?

Get the names of other mothers who use this childminder. Call them and get their opinions. Also ask your friends who use full-time childminders what they have found to be important.

It's important to take your time. Shop long and carefully. Try to avoid a situation in which you must make a panic decision or take the first person you find. Also, bear in mind the great value of keeping the same caretaker for as long as possible to minimize the adjustments your baby must make. The comment heard most often on this subject is "A good childminder makes all the difference in the world!"

Before we leave the subject of childminders we would like to discuss the issue of "wet-nursing". Occasionally a breastfeeding mother will seek out another lactating woman and ask her to breastfeed her baby while she works. Although some women have found this to be a workable alternative, please think carefully about it before you proceed. For one thing, the emotional overtones of breastfeeding are tremendous. Do you feel you can share this special relationship with a third person?

MAKING ARRANGEMENTS AT WORK

The first thing to be decided is whether your baby will receive formula or expressed breast milk while you are at work. Leaving formula with the sitter is a choice many women make to simplify their lives. It does not occur to some women that it is possible to combine breastfeeding and bottlefeeding in this way, but it is a very valid option. At first your breasts will feel full when you are away from your baby and you may need to express just a small amount of breast milk to relieve your discomfort. But remember, express only enough to relieve the feeling of being overly full, not enough to stimulate your milk supply. In a short time your body will adapt to the new situation. You'll find you have the right amount of milk at the right time.

The second choice, expressing breast milk to be left for the baby, requires greater planning and effort. But the women who choose this option find that the rewards outweigh the extra effort.

Once the decision is made, you will determine what arrangements you need to make at work. First, decide whether you have to discuss your plans with your boss. (You may have to make some special arrangements for your working day.) Next, think about when you will return to work. The longer you can stay at home with your baby, the easier it will be to manage breastfeeding and working, because your milk supply, your strength and your timetable will be better established. A year is better than six months, six months is better than three months, three months is better than six weeks, and even six weeks is better than four. You have to do what is most feasible in your own situation. Our information is often addressed specifically to the mother going back to work quite early, because she will have the more difficult time; other mothers can simply alter the information to fit their time schedules.

Do you have to make any changes in your work timetable? For example, Marilyn, who works as an educational consultant, and whose work is primarily independent of co-workers, made an agreement with her supervisor. "I discussed with my supervisor the fact that I would need to pump my breast milk at work. I told her that I would take the time I needed to pump and then add it back at the end of the day." This arrangement worked out to the satisfaction of both. Another breastfeeding mother, a social worker in private practice, simply locked her office door and pumped without anyone knowing about it. She also invested in a small refrigerator for her office to keep her breast milk cold.

Some other examples of adjustments in scheduling that one might make would be "flexi-time" (the freedom to arrange your hours according to your own convenience), or omitting lunch or breaks but taking time off to pump when necessary. Perhaps you can change your days off so that they don't coincide with your partner's, which will enable him to do more baby care. This way your baby gets great care and you save money on childminders, but there is a drawback to be considered. Many new parents find it very difficult to have pleasant times together, especially if they both work, and that feeling is certain to be intensified if days off are not spent together.

The place where you pump is also very important. Cindy, an administrative assistant in a university hospital, wanted to supply her baby with breast milk while he was at the childminder's. The only possible place she found for pumping was the employees' restroom and the only time was during lunch. The other workers complained so much about her monopolizing the restroom that she eventually had to give up her efforts.

What you need is a private place where you can pump for twenty to thirty minutes. If you work for a large institution, it could be very much worth your while to approach management or the personnel department and suggest that they purchase an electric breast pump for the employees' use. In any large group of workers, there are probably many women who would eventually take advantage of the pump. In addition to helping you, the purchase of a pump could also be very much to your employer's advantage. We can assume that a number of women will pump breast milk at work. Each of these women, then, will take less time away from her work if given the ease and convenience of an electric pump. In addition, because of the more thorough emptying of the breasts, there will be fewer days of work missed due to breast infections, and since it may encourage more mothers to breastfeed, there will probably be less time missed to look after babies who are ill. As we have pointed out, statistics show that breastfed babies tend to be ill less often than those receiving formula.

If you work for a small business in a large office building, you might investigate the possibility of a number of small businesses pooling their resources to purchase a breast pump for the entire building's use.

Before returning to work, many women feel considerable anxiety about what their co-workers will think of the idea of pumping breast milk at work. They fear that most people attach only sexual (rather than maternal) connotations to the breasts, and may feel uneasy about anything relating to the breasts and work. Another source of worry is how co-workers may feel about storing a body fluid at work. A woman who works in a public relations office shared the following anecdote with us:

> I had been feeling very self-conscious about storing the breast milk I pumped at work in the office refrigerator. I was hoping no one would ask me about it because I thought they might be revolted at the idea of having a body fluid stored in there with their food. I also thought my pumping might become a source of inappropriate joking. Finally that something I had dreaded happened. One day I got home and realized that I had forgotten to bring home my badly needed breast milk. I did not want to drive all the way back to the office. I only had one other choice. I knew that a young single man who lived near me was still at the office. I phoned him very apprehensively and explained the situation and asked him to bring me the milk. Much to my relief, rather than being revolted or snickering, he responded in a very pleasant and nonchalant way. He did not seem to think I had made a strange or exotic request. After this I was able to put others' perceptions of my storing breast milk into perspective.

I realized those fears had been within me and not based on objective facts from the outside.

Although these worries are normal, breastfeeding mothers usually find interest, support and encouragement at work, and their uncomfortable feelings quickly fade.

INVESTIGATING PUMPS

A very important issue to the working breastfeeding mother is that of breast pumps. Many women use hand expression exclusively, which generally works very well. If you wish to do this, see the discussion of hand expression in Chapter 4. If you are planning to use a breast pump, you need to look into the various types of pumps which are available.

The first category is the hand-held variety. One of the most common and inexpensive pumps is the type that looks like a bicycle horn. Most women find that it does not work well and can be uncomfortable and even painful to use. However, a few women, including one of our close friends, are successful with it. If you do decide to use this type of pump, apply a warm face flannel to your breast first to aid the let-down. Of course, be sure to read and follow the directions that come with the pump. The approximate cost at the time writing is £3 to £6.

We heard an interesting suggestion for use of the bicycle-horn-type pump which worked well for one woman, although we suspect it would not work for everyone. She attached one pump to her breast with suction, then simultaneously she pumped her other breast with a second pump. She claimed that she got large quantities of milk in a short amount of time; perhaps you will, too.

By far the most popular hand pump we have encountered is the cylindrical "piston" type, such as the Robbins Nurser (available from Boots), the AXicare Manual Breastpump Feeder or the Cannon Baby-safe Breastpump Feeding System. The Robbins and the AXicare ones extract milk straight into a feeding bottle, which forms part of the pump; the Cannon pumps the milk straight into a separate bottle. The teat with the Cannon version is the one which most resembles a human nipple. Prices range from just over £6 for the Robbins to £9 for the Cannon.

In general, most working/nursing women will need only a hand pump. It is still a good idea, though, to investigate the electric pumps. You may want to rent one for a limited amount of time to increase your milk supply, perhaps during the period right before you go back to work, or you may be able to afford to rent one full time.

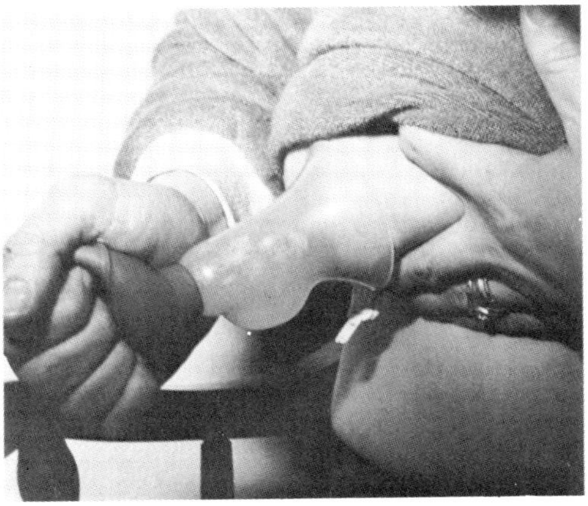

Although this bicycle-horn-type pump is the least expensive, most women find it to be the least desirable choice. (Photo by Harvey Schwartz)

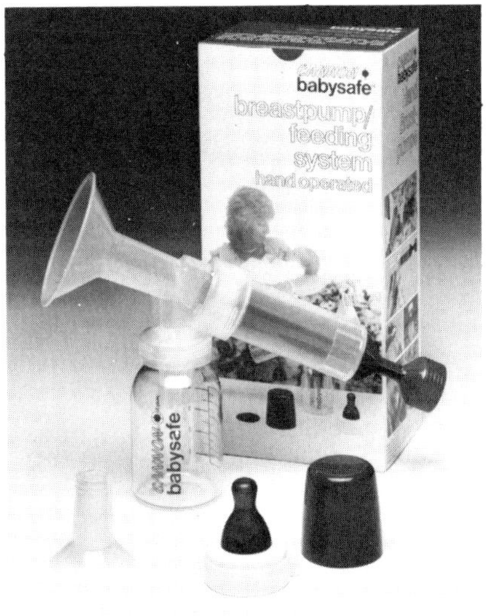

The Cannon Babysafe Breastpump Feeding System. (Courtesy of Cannon Rubber Ltd)

In addition to being the easiest way to pump, there are other advantages to an electric pump. Because it usually empties your breasts more thoroughly than hand-held pumps, you should be better able to maintain an adequate supply of milk. This more thorough emptying of your breasts will also help you to avoid breast infections.

Although hand expression and hand pumping both become quite easy with practice, there really is no easier way to pump your breasts than with an electric pump.

There are several electric breast pumps on the market, but we will discuss only two full-size pumps, the Egnell and the Medela. These pumps both have alternating suction, imitating a baby's sucking. They both have adjustable strength control and are very easy to work with. A word of caution: read the instructions that accompany the pump, and be careful until you are familiar with the pump and the amount of suction it creates.

The Medela is a relatively new pump which is very similar to the Egnell in principle. It is a little smaller and lighter. Since both of these pumps cost over £600, rental is the obvious option. The rental fee for both pumps will probably be about the same. Although it is not easy to transport an electric pump back and forth from work, it is certainly possible, for they are roughly the size and weight of a small portable sewing machine. It may be possible for you to leave the pump at work and use it only there.

For a Medela pump, contact La Leche League of Great Britain (see address list on p. 99). The cost: £10 deposit, £4.80 for the non-returnable parts, and 70p per day.

For an Egnell pump, contact the National Childbirth Trust or Egnell-Ameda Ltd. The cost is £8 for the first five days, including non-returnable items worth £3.50, and 90p per day thereafter.

Natural Joy also rent a pump, a small lightweight one at $3\frac{1}{2}$ lb, for 85p per day, kit £3.50, p & p £1.75, minimum charge £11.20. See the address list on p. 99.

There is a new small pump on the market which you could consider buying; the Mini Electric Breastpump from AXicare. This measures 4″×3″×2″, weighs $1\frac{1}{2}$ lb and fits into a handbag. It costs £59.95 plus £1.50 p & p, from Natural Joy.

There are some general guidelines to follow when pumping. When using a hand pump, moisten with warm water the part of the pump which will come into contact with the breast. If you are using an electric pump, you may find it helpful to gently massage the breast you are

An AXicare Manual Breastpump Feeder in use. (Courtesy of Natural Joy)

There is no denying that an electric pump is more expensive than any hand-held variety, but its advantage is that the process of emptying the breasts becomes virtually effortless. (Photo by Harvey Schwartz)

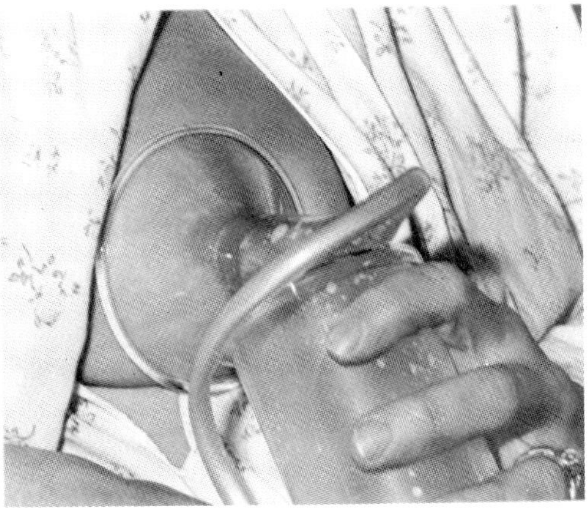

One convenience of an electric pump is that it requires only one hand, leaving the other one free. (Photo by Harvey Schwartz)

An electric pump kept at work is practical and convenient if you decide the expense is worthwhile. (Photo by Anne Price)

pumping with your free hand. With any type of pumping, go slowly and be gentle! If you are too full, express a little by hand before pumping. If you are not having success, take a break, relax and try again. Switch sides frequently, at least every three to five minutes. Think about your baby while you pump. You will be much more relaxed if you can find a private place in which to pump.

The most important thing to remember is that in order to be successful at pumping, you need a good supply. Make breastfeeding your baby your first priority, and feed frequently and for long periods whenever you are at home. So many other things, like housework and your social life, will always be there, but this breastfeeding period in your life will be yours for just a short time.

You should be aware that if you are working full time and want to leave breast milk for your baby, it is possible that you may not be able to pump enough milk to keep up with your baby's needs. In this case, you may want to keep in mind that the major benefit of your continued breastfeeding is to have that emotionally fulfilling experience available to you and your baby during the time you are together. If you think of this as your goal, rather than never having a drop of formula pass your baby's lips, you will find the whole experience more pleasant and less anxiety-producing. If you leave some formula at the childminder's as an emergency back-up, you will probably find yourself less pressured and less worried about your baby's hunger.

When choosing formula, discuss it with your doctor or health visitor. Also keep in mind that cow's-milk formula is more nutritious than soy formula, and that almost as many babies are allergic to soy as to cow's milk. Start with a milk formula and consider a soy-based one only if problems occur. If you are planning to leave formula, try it a couple of times *before* you go back to work to make sure the baby doesn't have a bad reaction to it. Since you know what's normal for your baby, you are the best one to assess whether your baby's behaviour constitutes a bad reaction.

INTRODUCING BOTTLES

Another area of pressing concern to a new mother who knows she will soon be returning to work is getting the baby to accept the bottle. There is no thought more disturbing to a mother than to think of her baby shrieking with hunger and unable to eat. For your peace of mind, you must be sure that your baby will eat at the childminder's while you are gone.

The two smallest pumps in the AXicare line seem to be nearly ideal for women who choose to invest in the convenience of an electric pump.

(Photos by All Photographic Services)

The age at which it is best to begin introducing the bottle depends a great deal on how much time you have before going back to work. In general, you probably won't want to introduce a bottle before six weeks. Six weeks is the time it usually takes for a woman's milk supply to become stabilized, so if at all possible, wait until then. If you must return to work earlier than six weeks, you can wait until just before you return to introduce the bottle.

How often should you give the baby a bottle? If you are returning to work within a few weeks, you will want the baby to have one bottle every few days. If you have more time at home, it could be one bottle a week or even less. It is important for your milk supply that you don't overdo this.

You need to decide what types of bottles to use. There has been some research which indicates that storing breast milk in either glass or soft plastic containers may slightly impair the immunological value of the milk, and so a hard plastic bottle looks like a better choice for storage. Whatever you choose, you must obtain quite a large number of bottles. The four-ounce ones are a good idea, since you will want to freeze in small quantities.

Next, you need to select a teat. Many mothers find that the baby can switch back and forth from bottle to breast with less confusion if a Playtex Nurser is used because the teat on this is more breast-shaped than others. The Playtex Nurser uses disposable plastic bags for the milk and is available at Boots for around £3. A teat which fits ordinary bottles and looks more nipple-like than most is "Nu-flo" by Cannon-Babysafe. If your baby doesn't seem to like those, it may be that he won't object to ordinary teats.

How do you introduce the bottle to the baby? At this point, you want your baby to accept the bottle, but you also want to build your milk supply. For this reason, we recommend that you anticipate a time when the baby would normally breastfeed. Pump your breasts (just a little while before you anticipate the baby's hunger), put that milk into a bottle and use it immediately. If the baby is fed before he is *extremely* hungry, he may be more cooperative about trying something new.

Someone other than the mother should give the baby the bottle. The baby is more likely to accept it from someone else, because he associates the mother with the pleasant sensations connected with feeding at her breast and may fight getting the milk any other way. This, however, is an advantage and something to be reinforced. Since one of the risks of breastfeeding and working is that the baby may reject the breast for the bottle, the association of the mother with the breast exclusively is very

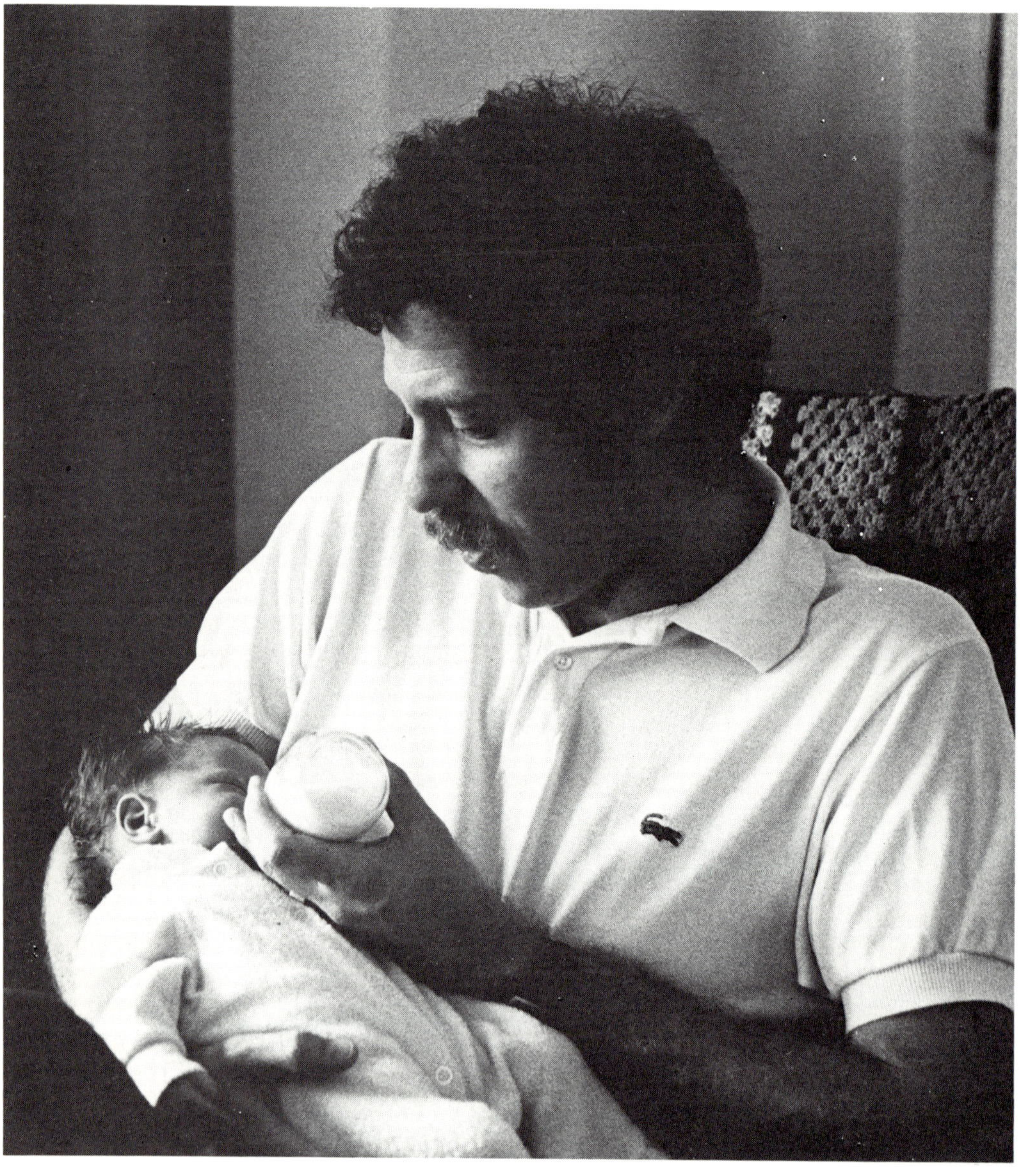

An important element in preparing to go back to work is helping your baby adjust to accepting some feeds from a bottle. (Photo by Anne Price)

helpful. The father is the most logical person to give the bottle. However, if that isn't possible, someone else who feels confident and patient with the baby should be chosen.

A problem which most women will never face, but which we feel we should address anyway, is the baby's refusal of the bottle. There are several possible strategies for dealing with this. Perhaps the teat is being pushed into the baby's mouth too aggressively. Try laying the teat next to the baby's mouth and letting him grasp it himself. It is also possible that another type of teat would be more to your baby's liking. Some babies are amazingly opinionated—try them all.

Something else to remember is that the nipple your baby is used to is at body temperature, and the one which is now being offered may be cold. Try running warm water over the bottle teat before offering it to the baby. This has been especially helpful in many cases.

The hole in the teat may be too large or too small. Hold the bottle upside down and see if the milk pours out or if, even after squeezing the teat vigorously, only a drop appears. Both situations can be very frustrating to the baby. If the hole is too big, change teats; if it is too small, use a red-hot pin and poke a bigger one. If all else fails and your baby absolutely refuses the bottle, the childminder can get nourishment into him with either a spoon or an eyedropper. She should continue to offer the bottle, and the baby will probably give in shortly.

STARTING TO STORE MILK

It is important to have a little stockpile of breast milk before you go back to work, for your own peace of mind and to compensate for a day when you may pump less. When should you begin to store breast milk in anticipation of returning to work? If you will be using a freezer which is part of a refrigerator rather than a deep freeze (which goes below zero degrees Fahrenheit), you don't have to begin to store milk until two weeks before you go back to work, because frozen milk will not keep longer than two weeks unless it is kept below zero, and most freezer compartments in refrigerators don't get that cold. When you begin to store milk, reread and carefully follow the procedure outlined in Chapter 4.

If you do have access to a deep freeze, you might begin to store three or four weeks before returning to work, if you have time. A good idea, which one mother used, was to rent a good electric pump (see p. 40) for one month prior to returning to work. She had the double benefit of accumulating a stockpile of frozen milk in the easiest way possible, and she also built up her supply by emptying her breasts more thoroughly. Remember, though, this period at home with your baby is short. Don't let anxiety about storing milk interfere with the pleasure of breast-feeding your baby.

FINAL COUNTDOWN

It is about a week before you will return to work. You have hired a childminder, you have made all the necessary arrangements at work, and you have some breast milk stored in the freezer. Now comes your "trial run" period.

It would be unfortunate if your baby's first contact with his caretaker were on your first full day of work. Your baby should have at least a slight familiarity with his new surroundings on his first full day. About a week before your first day back at work, make arrangements to leave your baby with his new caretaker for a short amount of time which does not include a feed. Try an hour or an hour and a half. A few days later, arrange to leave the baby for a couple of hours, including a feeding time. This will give your childminder a chance to thaw and give a bottle of breast milk while thoroughly following your detailed instructions. You should be available for a telephone conversation to answer questions or discuss problems. Now you will be able to leave your baby when you return to work without immersing him suddenly into an environment which is one hundred percent strange. You'll feel less stressed and better able to handle your first days at work.

4/Handling Breast Milk

THERE MAY BE many reasons for a woman to feel it is important to leave breast milk, rather than formula, for her baby while she is working. The baby may be allergic or sensitive to formula. (This is more common than many people realize.) She may have some digestive difficulties. The mother may feel that it is a way of nurturing which is important to both of them. She may not want her baby to miss the many nutritional benefits a breastfed baby receives. The questions we face now are how to express the milk, how to store it until the baby takes it, and how to thaw it properly to allow the least bacterial growth.

PUMPING

Let's address the issue of pumping first. You need to decide what type of pumping you will be doing: hand expression, using a hand pump or using an electric pump. You will probably want to try several alternatives and decide which one works best for you.

We talk about the different types of electric and hand pumps in Chapter 3. However, many women, even those who work full time, find that hand expression is their preferred method. It is easy, convenient and effective once you have mastered it, although in the beginning it may be awkward and slow. We will present two methods of hand expression. Both work well. Try both and see which one you find more comfortable. The first technique we'll outline was developed by long-time La Leche League leader, Jo Ann Touchton, who has great expertise in the areas of hand expression and sucking problems.

Before you begin to hand express, it is important to wash your hands well. Support your breast with the opposite hand (left breast with right hand and vice-versa), the heel of your palm resting against your ribs. Then place your first and second fingers about one-and-a-half inches

Although it takes a little time to get the knack of hand expression, it is an art worth learning. Many women who master this technique find it to be their preferred method of pumping. (Photo by Harvey Schwartz)

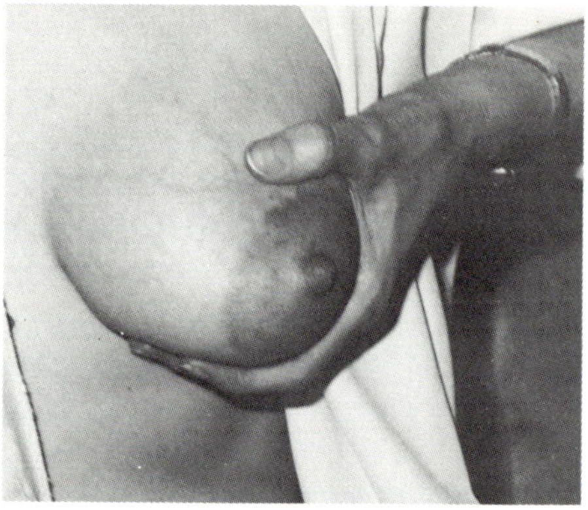

This woman's fingers are placed at the point where she located her lactiferous sinuses. Remember, the location of your sinuses is not necessarily at the outer edge of the areola, since areola size varies from one woman to another. (Photo by Harvey Schwartz)

back from your nipple in a scissors position. This is about where your lactiferous sinuses are (see the diagram on p. 17 in Chapter 2). You may have to experiment and move either forwards or backwards a little from this point to obtain the best results. Squeeze your fingers together and release a few times. (Press them together like pliers, straight and true, not like scissors, which would cross and kink. It should never feel like a pinch.) Then rotate your hand to another point and repeat the process. Continue rotating all around the areola, as if moving around a clock, until you have pumped all areas of the breast. You will have to change hands. Once you have a feel for how much pressure you should be using in the scissors position, you can use your thumb on the top and your middle finger on the bottom. This is much less awkward, but be cautious! It is a mistake to use strong pressure or to squeeze the whole breast with your hand. This can cause pressure in a duct system and can lead to a breast infection.

If you don't seem to be getting much milk after a few minutes of using one of these procedures, perhaps you are not pumping at the right points. There is a technique, also developed by Jo Ann Touchton, for finding your lactiferous sinuses—this is where you should be pumping. You can locate your sinuses by walking with your fingers backwards from the tip of the nipple towards the breast. At the tip and just behind, it feels like smooth tissue. About a half to one-and-a-half inches back there is an area which feels like small lumps—these are the lactiferous sinuses. Your fingers should be just at the back of or on top of them.

With any pumping method, you will find that switching breasts every few minutes will increase your effectiveness. This allows the milk to come down and collect in the sinuses of the breast you are not pumping. You may also find it helpful to hold the clean glass container into which you are pumping between your legs and lean over it as you pump. This leaves both hands free to alternate pumping, and the effect of gravity should help. A one-pint measuring jug works well for this because of its wide mouth.

A similar method of hand expression is called the Marmet Technique. This technique has been thoroughly developed and well explained by Chele Marmet herself in La Leche League Reprint No. 107.[1] We feel her information is very complete and important to any woman who wants to learn the art of hand expression.

Another consideration if you intend to pump at work is an appropriate wardrobe. Basically, you need two-piece outfits or something that buttons in front. With a little experimentation you will certainly be able to find clothes that are appropriate for work and which facilitate pumping.

You'll need to determine how often you need to or are able to pump at work. Some women find it best to pump at about the same time the baby would be breastfeeding. An educational consultant we know told us, "I find that to get a let-down consistently and keep my supply up, I need to pump at the same times my baby would normally feed." However, others find that their let-downs can be easily programmed to the new routine of breaks and lunchtime.

Some women pump at lunch and at a break, or twice a day; others pump only at lunch. This will be determined partly by how much milk you can get each time and partly by how flexible your timetable is. For example, one woman pumps eight ounces of breast milk a day. She says, "I found that I had the most milk in the morning and late at night. So I pumped about two ounces right after his first feed in the morning, four ounces during my lunch hour, and two more ounces just before bed." Incidentally, most women usually have more milk at these times of the day.

[1]© 1978, revised 1979, 1981, Chele Marmet. Reprinted with permission of The Lactation Institute, West Los Angeles, California.

THE LACTATION INSTITUTE

and Breastfeeding Clinic

3441 Clairton Place, Encino California 91436
(213) 995-1913

Manual Expression of Breast Milk

MARMET TECHNIQUE

The Marmet Technique of manual expression and assisting the let-down reflex has worked for hundreds of mothers – in a way that nothing has before. Even experienced breastfeeding mothers who have been able to hand express will find that this method produces more milk. Mothers who have previously been able to express only a small amount, or none at all, get excellent results with this technique.

TECHNIQUE IS IMPORTANT

When watching manual expression the correct milking motion is difficult to see. In this case the hand is quicker than the eye. Consequently, many mothers have found manual expression difficult – even after watching a demonstration or reading a brief description. Milk can be expressed when using less effective methods of hand expressions. When used, however, on a frequent and regular basis, these methods can easily lead to damaged breast tissue, bruised breasts, and even skin burns.

The Marmet technique of manual expression was developed by a mother who needed to express her milk over an extended period of time for medical reasons. She found that her let-down reflex did not work as well as when her baby nursed, so she also developed a method of massage and stimulation to assist her let-down. The key to the success of this technique is the combination of the method of expression and this massage.

This technique is effective and should not cause problems. It can easily be learned by following this step by step guide. As with any manual skill, practice is important.

ADVANTAGES

There are many advantages to manual expression over mechanical methods of milking the breasts:

- Some mechanical pumps cause discomfort and are ineffective.
- Many mothers are more comfortable with manual expression of breast milk because it is more natural.
- Skin-to-skin contact is more stimulating than the feel of a plastic shield. So manual expression usually allows for easier let-down.
- It's convenient.
- It's ecologically superior.
- It's portable. How can a mother forget her hands?
- Best of all it's free!

MARMET TECHNIQUE OF MANUAL EXPRESSION OF BREAST MILK

HOW THE BREAST WORKS

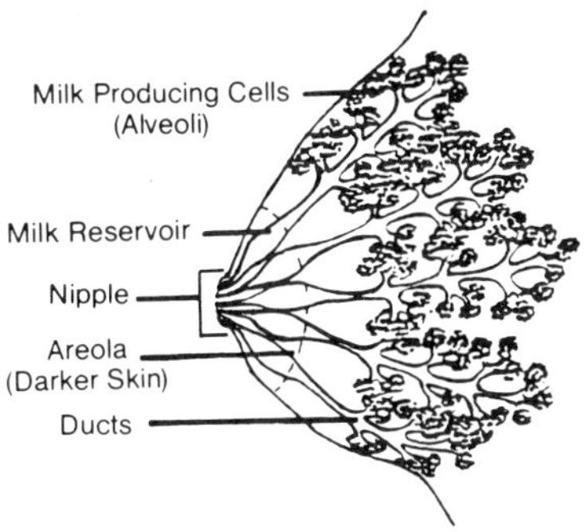

The milk is produced in milk producing cells (alveoli). A portion of the milk continuously comes down the ducts and collects in the milk reservoirs. When the milk-producing cells are stimulated, they expel additional milk into the duct system (let-down reflex).

EXPRESSING THE MILK

Draining The Milk Reservoirs

1. **POSITION** the thumb and first two fingers about **1" to 1½" behind the nipple.**

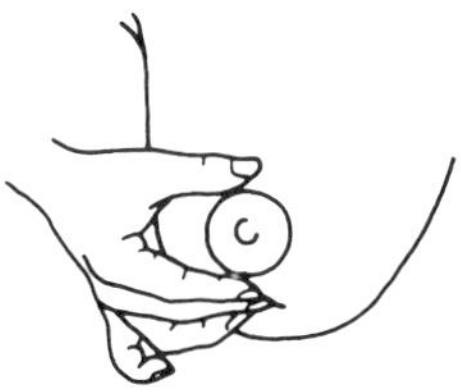

- Use this measurement, which is not necessarily the outer edge of the areola, as a guide. The areola varies in size from one woman to another.

- Place the thumb above the nipple and the fingers below as shown.

- Note that the fingers are positioned so that the milk reservoirs lie beneath them.

- Avoid cupping the breast.

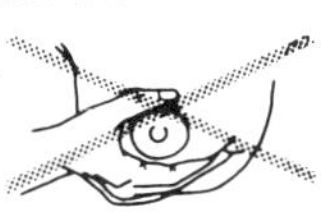

2. **PUSH** straight into the chest wall.

- Avoid spreading the fingers apart.

- For large breasts, first lift and then push into the chest wall.

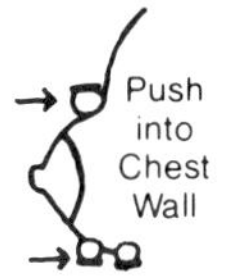

3. **ROLL** thumb and fingers forward as if making thumb and fingerprints at the same time.

- The **rolling motion** of the thumb and fingers compresses and empties the milk reservoirs without hurting sensitive breast tissue.

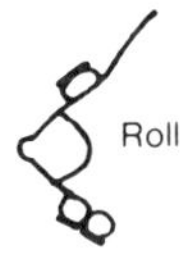

- Note the moving position of the thumbnail and fingernails in illustration.

4. **REPEAT RHYTHMICALLY** to drain the reservoirs.

- Position, push, roll; position, push, roll . . .

5. **ROTATE** the thumb and finger position to milk the other reservoirs. Use both hands on each breast. These pictures show hand positions on the right breast.

Right Hand **Left Hand**

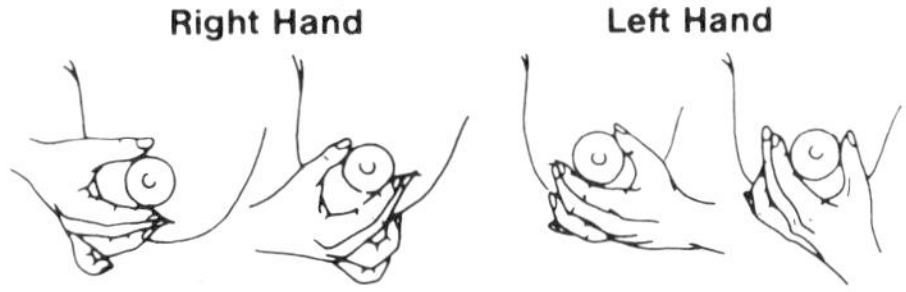

AVOID THESE MOTIONS

Avoid squeezing the breast. This can cause bruising.

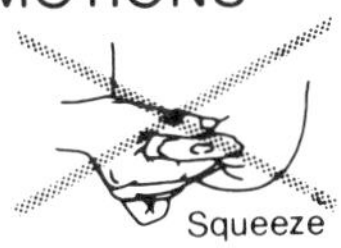

Avoid pulling out the nipple and breast. This can cause tissue damage.

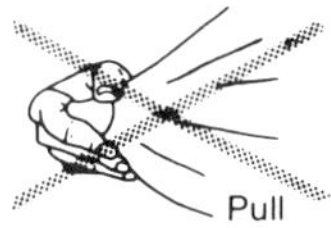

Avoid sliding on the breast. This can cause skin burns.

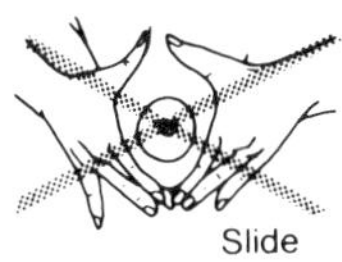

MARMET TECHNIQUE OF MANUAL EXPRESSION OF BREAST MILK

ASSISTING THE LET-DOWN

Stimulating The Flow Of Milk

1. **MASSAGE** the milk producing cells and ducts.

- Start at the top of the breast. Press firmly into the chest wall. Move fingers in a circular motion on one spot on the skin.

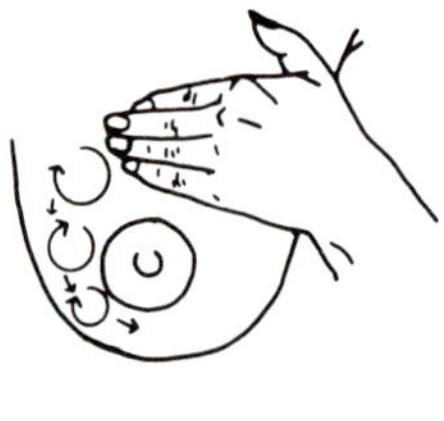

MASSAGE

- After a few seconds move the fingers to the next area on the breast.

- **Spiral** around the breast toward the areola using this massage.

- The motion is similar to that used in a breast examination.

2. **STROKE** the breast area from the top of the breast to the nipple with a light **tickle-like stroke.**

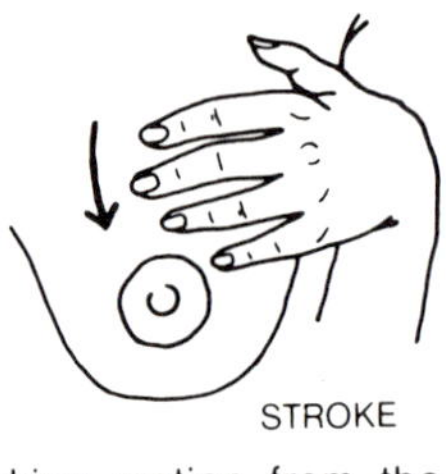

STROKE

- Continue this stroking motion from the chest wall to the nipple around the whole breast.

- This will help with relaxation and will help stimulate the let-down reflex.

3. **SHAKE** the breast while leaning forward so that gravity will help the milk let-down.

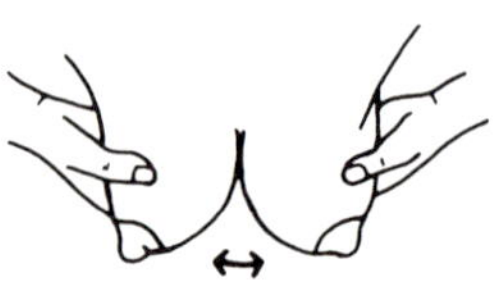

SHAKE

PROCEDURE

This procedure should be followed by mothers who are expressing in place of a full feeding and those who need to establish, increase, or maintain their milk supply when the baby cannot nurse.

- Express each breast until the flow of milk slows down.

- Assist the let-down (massage, stroke, shake) on both breasts. This can be done simultaneously.

- Repeat the whole process of expressing each breast and assisting the let-down once or twice more. The flow of milk usually slows down sooner the second and third time as the reservoirs are drained.

TIMING

The ENTIRE PROCEDURE should take approximately 20-30 MINUTES.

- Express each breast 5-7 minutes.
- Massage, stroke, shake.
- Express each breast 3-5 minutes.
- Massage, stroke, shake.
- Express each breast 2-3 minutes.

Note: If the milk supply is established, use the times given only as a guide. Watch the flow of milk and change breasts when the flow gets small.

Note: If little or no milk is present yet, follow these suggested times closely.

A pumping will usually take around twenty minutes. This varies significantly, of course, depending on how much milk you need to pump. If you alternate breasts frequently you will probably get more milk. Don't be discouraged if, in the beginning, you get very little milk when you pump. When you are just learning to pump, you may get less than an ounce at a time. Once you are really proficient, you may get as much as eight ounces at one sitting, although many women get less.

In order to get your milk out effectively, you must have a let-down. Remember some women never feel any particular sensation when they let down, while others feel a tingling or even a mild ache. You do not need to *feel* one to *have* one.

If you have trouble getting a let-down, try stimulating your nipple before you pump. One woman, a nurse, wets her fingers with warm water and pulls gently on her nipples to aid the let-down. The sensation is probably reminiscent of her baby's mouth on her breast. It is also helpful to have a quiet place where you are comfortable enough to relax. Your mental set is important, so take a moment to get out of your "employee" frame of mind and into a "mother" frame of mind. Try your childbirth education relaxation techniques for a minute or two. Then think of your baby, how she looks, how she feels, how she smells and sounds. Some women even look at a picture of the baby while they pump. One woman looks at a picture of herself breastfeeding her baby!

A woman who is experiencing severe problems with let-down can ask her doctor about Syntocinon. This is artificial oxytocin, the let-down hormone. It comes in a nasal spray and will help to induce a let-down. Many women are successful with only half a dose. But do try other methods first and use Syntocinon only as a last resort. Repeated use is not recommended because it can cause a rebound effect.

Many women pump only at work, but there are women who feel they cannot meet their baby's requirements if they don't pump at home as well. Some women take this pumping concern too far. When they pump at home, they pump immediately *before* they feed the baby because they are so concerned about getting a large amount of milk for the bottle. This sets up an unfortunate competition. Sucking on a partially empty breast is a frustrating and unsatisfying experience for the baby. On the other hand, when she gets the bottle, the milk flows easily and plentifully. No wonder a baby facing this choice soon chooses the bottle! So if you need to pump at home, there should be no problem as long as you breastfeed the baby *first*.

The practice of pumping for a bottle before you breastfeed could defeat your original intentions. Do you want to provide your baby with a pleasurable and satisfying experience at the breast and perhaps supplement with formula occasionally, or leave only breast milk in the bottle but offer the baby frustration at the breast? You may need to reassure yourself once in a while and remember that the mothering you do is almost always more important than the substance that goes into your baby's stomach.

For your own health and well-being, and also for your milk supply, you need to take care of yourself as well as your baby. Keep high-protein and nutritious snacks, like nuts or dried fruit, where they are easily accessible—in your car, handbag and desk. You may want to take a good vitamin supplement. You can also make a high-protein drink for breakfast or take it to work in a thermos. Also remember to keep your fluid intake high while you're working.

As difficult as it may be, you must try to get as much extra rest as you can. Try to go to bed as early as possible. You can minimize lost sleep by bringing the baby into your bed for night feeds and then just going back to sleep with her. (No, you won't roll over on her!) Napping with the baby at the weekend is another good idea. In every way possible, try not to overload yourself during this special time of your life.

Remember, even though you may not wean for some time, a point will come when you will either no longer need to pump at work, or you will become less willing to continue. At some time during the second half of the first year, your baby will probably be taking juice and a significant amount of food and will soon be drinking cow's milk. You may feel that you no longer need to supply any breast milk for your baby while she is at the childminder's. Or you may feel that one bottle, which you can supply by pumping at home, is sufficient.

Your feelings may also change during the course of the breastfeeding relationship. In the beginning, you will probably feel very committed to pumping your milk at work, partly because it is a way for you to feel that you are mothering your baby during that time. At some later point, as you recognize that your baby's physical need for breast milk is lessening, you may feel your own social needs becoming more important. You may begin to miss having lunch with your peers and may forego pumping at that time. Rather than offering a timetable stating how long you can expect to continue pumping during your lunch hour at work, we recommend that you let your perceptions of both your needs and your baby's needs be your guide.

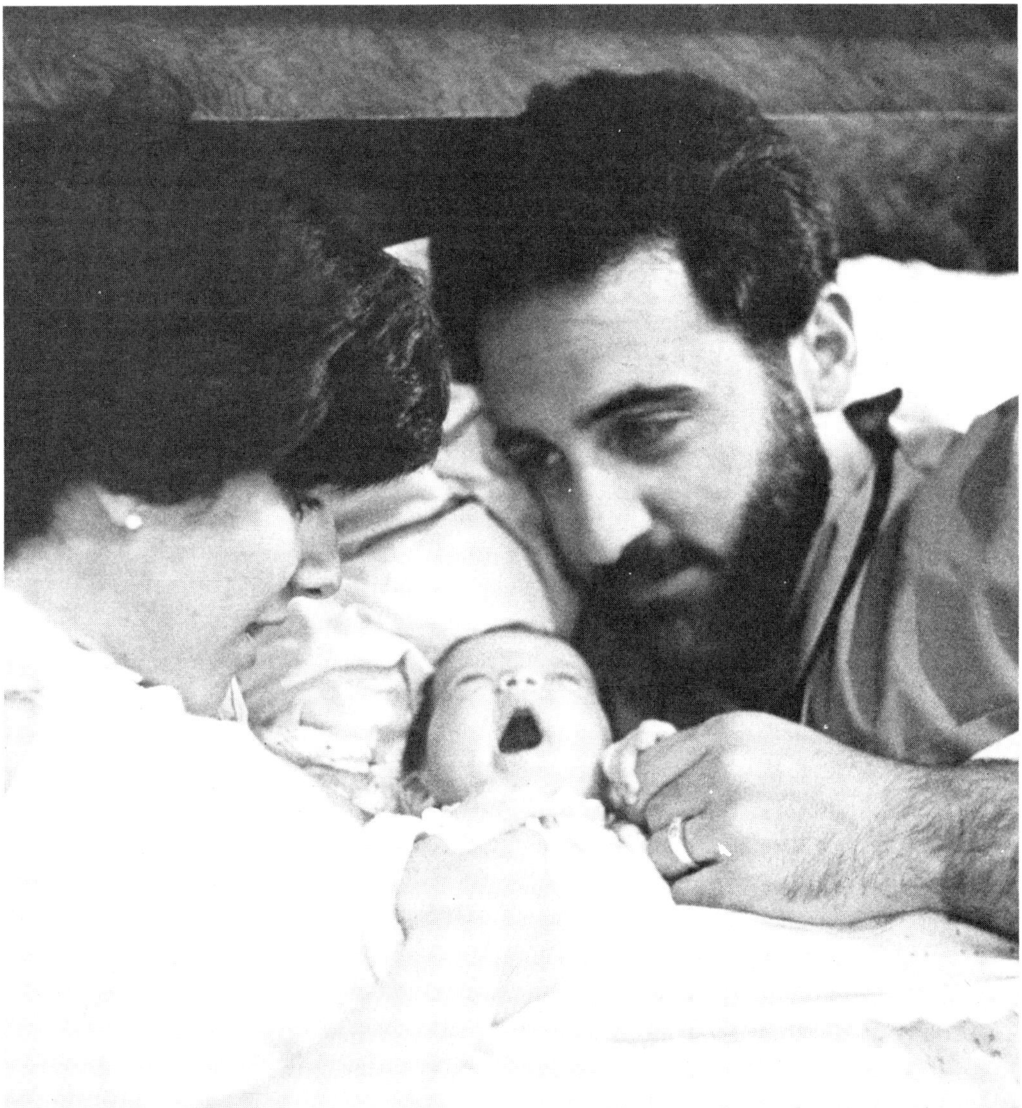

A way to increase physical contact and cuddling time for your whole family is to bring your baby into bed with you. And everyone gets more rest this way, too. (Photo by Anne Price)

STORING

If you are going to be storing breast milk, you will need to learn some basic facts about how to keep it safely. Remember, expressed breast milk contains some bacteria from your skin which can multiply over time if not stored correctly. If you accidentally give your baby spoiled breast milk, it will result in vomiting and diarrhoea.

If you have a dishwasher, it is a good idea to clean the bottles in it; otherwise hot water and soap will do. If you want to sterilize them, the water in your dishwasher must reach one hundred and eighty degrees Fahrenheit. Otherwise you must boil the bottles for twenty to twenty-five minutes, or use a chemical sterilizer like Milton. It's a good idea to rinse sterilizing fluid off bottles and teats with boiled water before using them again.

After you pump your milk into a clean container, pour it into the bottle. If milk will be added to previously frozen milk, put it in the back of the refrigerator, with a lid on it, to cool for half an hour before pouring it on top of the frozen milk. If warm milk were poured on top of frozen milk a layer would defrost and refreeze. Breast milk should never be *re*frozen.

If the milk will be used within forty-eight hours, you can keep it in the refrigerator. If you won't be using it that soon, freeze it and mark it with the date, and use the oldest milk first. You can pour cooled milk into an older bottle to get the number of ounces you desire, but if you mix new milk with old, go by the old date.

A nurse in Denver came up with a creative idea. She froze some of her milk in plastic ice cube trays. She was careful that the milk all came from about the same period of time and was sure not to pour warm milk on frozen. She kept the tray covered with cling film and dated it. Each cube equalled about one ounce. Once they were frozen, she popped them into a plastic bag and dated it. This worked out well for her because the bag of cubes was kept at her childminder's, and if her son was not quite satisfied with his feed or if he became hungry just before she returned from the hospital, milk was available in small quantities, and it wasn't necessary to defrost an entire new bottle.

Breast milk can be kept frozen in the freezer compartment of a refrigerator for two weeks. It can be kept for up to two years in a deep freeze which goes below zero degrees Fahrenheit. Once breast milk is thawed, it is not as bacteria-resistant, so it can be kept in the refrigerator only three or four hours. You may want to hold it a maximum of three hours for a newborn and four hours for an older baby.

However, it is absolutely best to give the baby the fresh milk you pump the following day, and supplement only if necessary with frozen milk. This is because frozen breast milk has lost antibodies, and some of the nutrients can no longer be absorbed by the baby's system. If only a minority of your baby's feeds consist of frozen milk, this is not a major concern. After all, formula doesn't contain any antibodies.

When you pump your milk at work, you need to be very careful with its storage. Try to find a refrigerator to store it in at work. If your place of work does not have a refrigerator, you can suggest that your co-workers chip in and buy a small one. Everyone would benefit by being able to keep lunches, snacks and drinks in it.

One word of caution at this point: if you have considered wearing plastic breast shields at work and saving the milk that leaks into them, don't do it. It is not safe to keep breast milk at room temperature or body temperature. You could end up making your baby ill by giving her spoiled milk.

TRANSPORTING

It really makes the most sense for you to drop milk off at the childminder's the same day you pump it if it is to be used fresh the next day. If you are planning to freeze it, you can do so at the minder's house (remember to date it). Cutting down on transportation of the milk will be easier for you and will reduce the possibility of spoilage.

You can carry your milk home or to the childminder's in an insulated container or "Cool Box", with ice packs to keep it cold. Different types of container vary in their effectiveness, so you should experiment to find the best way of keeping your bags or bottles of milk as cold as possible. Make sure that the container still feels really cold when you arrive. It is inconvenient to have to refreeze the ice packs each day, but it is effective with either fresh or frozen milk.

If you come up with another travel idea for your milk, test it to see if it is effective. If you are transporting refrigerated milk, you can put an indoor/outdoor thermometer in the milk container and check to see that it stays between zero degrees and thirty-two degrees Fahrenheit.

If you are transporting frozen milk, it is very important for it to stay completely frozen. Thawing could lead to refreezing, and that is always to be avoided. If you should discover that your milk has begun to thaw, you must finish thawing it under running water and use it within four hours, or throw it away.

Transporting your milk will not be as complicated a matter as it may seem. You will arrive at a method which is easy for you and it will become part of your routine. Our aim in this discussion is not to make it sound difficult, but to point out the safety factors involved with transporting raw milk.

THAWING

Now that you have taken steps to pump, store and transport your breast milk under safe conditions, leave your childminder with very specific instructions about thawing and warming the milk. This is important. If the milk is fresh, she must keep it in the refrigerator until just before she uses it. When she warms it, she can do it either under running tap water or in a pan of water on the stove. She should not overheat it. Also make sure she never sets the bottle out at room temperature to warm. Breast milk cannot remain unrefrigerated that long.

If she is using frozen breast milk, she cannot set it out to thaw. To thaw frozen breast milk, hold the bottle under cool, running tap water, gradually changing it from cool to tepid to warm. She can continue to warm the bottle under tap water or, once the milk is all liquid, she can heat it in a pan of water on the stove. She *cannot* thaw frozen breast milk on the stove. It will curdle and be undrinkable.

Again, once a bottle of frozen milk has been thawed, it is good for only three to four hours in the refrigerator. If the baby does not finish it during that time, it must be discarded.

These guidelines are important for your baby's safety. Once you have established a routine, you will probably not find them complicated or inconvenient.

TIMES TO REMEMBER

30 Minutes
Cool breast milk in refrigerator before adding to previously frozen milk.

3–4 Hours
Thawed breast milk is safe if kept refrigerated.

24–48 Hours
Fresh breast milk is safe if kept refrigerated.

2 Weeks
Frozen breast milk is safe in freezer compartment of average refrigerator.

2 Years
Frozen breast milk is safe if kept below zero degrees Fahrenheit, as in deep freeze.

THAWING BREAST MILK

Run bottle of frozen breast milk under running tap water, first cool, then tepid, then warm.

NEVER LET IT STAND AT ROOM TEMPERATURE!

NEVER HEAT IT UNLESS IT IS FIRST COMPLETELY THAWED AND LIQUID!

ALWAYS HEAT IT SLOWLY AND GENTLY!

5/Difficulties

As we begin this discussion of the most common difficulties, let us assure you that you will certainly not experience all the problems mentioned here, and that you may very well not experience any of them. By the time your baby is six weeks old, you will probably be past most difficulties and totally enjoying your breastfeeding experience.

There are certain things you can expect during the hospital stay after your baby is born. One is an exaggerated emotional state, due to hormonal changes. This can make any small problem or negative comment seem much worse than it really is. Many women find that they cry very easily during this period. We know of one woman who cried when the nurse criticized the way in which she wrapped her baby in his blanket. Another friend sobbed at great length when she was told that her newborn daughter was jaundiced, although this is a common and generally not serious condition.

GETTING BABY ON/OFF THE BREAST

Often, the first difficulty a new mother faces is getting the baby on and off the breast properly. Use the guideline offered in Chapter 2 to get the baby on the breast. If the baby does not open his mouth wide enough, take him off and do it again until he is on the breast correctly. You do not want your baby to get used to feeding in an incorrect position even briefly. It could lead to sucking problems and slow weight gain. Most babies adopt the proper position quite naturally, but even if you have to work with your baby a little in the beginning, his positioning will become automatic before you know it.

To get the baby off the breast, you can wait until he falls asleep or lets go. Or, if you want to take the baby off or switch sides while he is still sucking, slip your finger into his mouth to break the suction and then take him off. Never just pull the baby off. It will hurt you. We heard of one woman who hadn't discovered this painless way of getting the baby off the breast until her fifth baby!

ENGORGEMENT

Your milk will come in between the second and the fifth days. When it comes in, you may experience engorgement, especially if it is your first baby. Engorgement is extreme fullness and tightness in your breasts. Some of this fullness is due to extra blood volume in your breast tissue and some of it to milk. The reason you become engorged is that your baby has not yet programmed the milk-making mechanism within your breasts. You have too much milk because your breasts don't yet know how much your baby needs. Engorgement will be less of a problem for you if you try not to limit your baby's sucking time. Feed as often and as long as your baby likes. Engorgement usually goes away in a few days, once your baby has been feeding and sending the correct "supply messages". However, you may continue to get very full and leak before each feed for several weeks.

During the period of engorgement you may need to hand-express some milk before your baby begins to feed, in order to soften the areola a little so the baby can get it into his mouth. Express only enough to relieve the overfullness. If you express too much you will be tampering with the supply-and-demand system.

Also be aware that engorgement can lead to sore nipples if not handled carefully. Andrea T. told us:

> I was incredibly engorged during the first couple of weeks of Evan's life. My breasts were just huge and hard as rocks. I was really shocked by their condition. Poor Evan! He would be hungry and try to suck, but since my breasts were so large and hard, he could get very little but my nipple into his mouth. Naturally I really got sore. I didn't get better until I started expressing a little milk by hand before I fed him so he could get more into his mouth.

At this point, with so much milk, you may find that your baby gulps loudly (getting some air, too) or even chokes, unable to keep up with the forceful spray of milk. There may be increased spitting-up or wind. If this happens, try to take your baby off the breast during the initial part of the let-down and let the milk spray into a handkerchief or tissue. After the "big spray" is over, put him back on. Once your baby is a little

A new baby sometimes needs to be taught to get onto the breast, but an older baby like this one will latch on efficiently all by herself. (Photo by Harvey Schwartz)

older, he will be able to keep up with the let-down of your milk.

SORE NIPPLES

Another problem you may experience is sore nipples. Hopefully you followed our suggestions for preventing nipple soreness (see Chapter 2), but if you have them anyway, here's what to do. First and foremost, check the baby's feeding position, making sure you have him on correctly and that his mouth is open wide and his bottom lip is curled outward. Alternate feeding positions between sitting up and lying down. Air-dry your nipples after each feed, then apply a thin layer of pure lanolin. If you apply anything to your sore nipples, try to wipe off the excess before feeding your baby.

We know of one maternity nurse who claims to have helped many new mothers recover from sore nipples by using lip salve on them. This makes some sense, because the skin on your nipples is much like that on your lips. A remedy used in some hospitals is putting damp teabags on the nipples. The tannic acid seems to be helpful. You can also use icepacks to relieve pain. If none of these remedies helps you, try simply exposing your nipples to air!

Remember, never wash your nipples with soap, alcohol or sprays. Just letting the water in the shower or bath run over them is enough. Nature has provided little glands on your areola which serve as cleansers. They may look like little bumps and are called Montgomery glands.

PLUGGED DUCTS AND BREAST INFECTIONS

Problems which may be slightly more common among working/breastfeeding mothers than among nonemployed breastfeeding mothers are plugged ducts and breast infections. A plugged duct is just what the name implies. You know you have one when there is a sore, inflamed, hard spot on your breast. If you discover one, apply heat to that spot, try to find a way to get extra rest, and feed on that side first. You need to keep the affected side as empty as possible and again it is helpful to vary positions. Also try gently massaging that spot while feeding.

If you do not solve the problem while it is just a plugged duct, a fever will probably develop and you will feel as if you have the flu. At this point the condition may have developed into a breast infection. Call

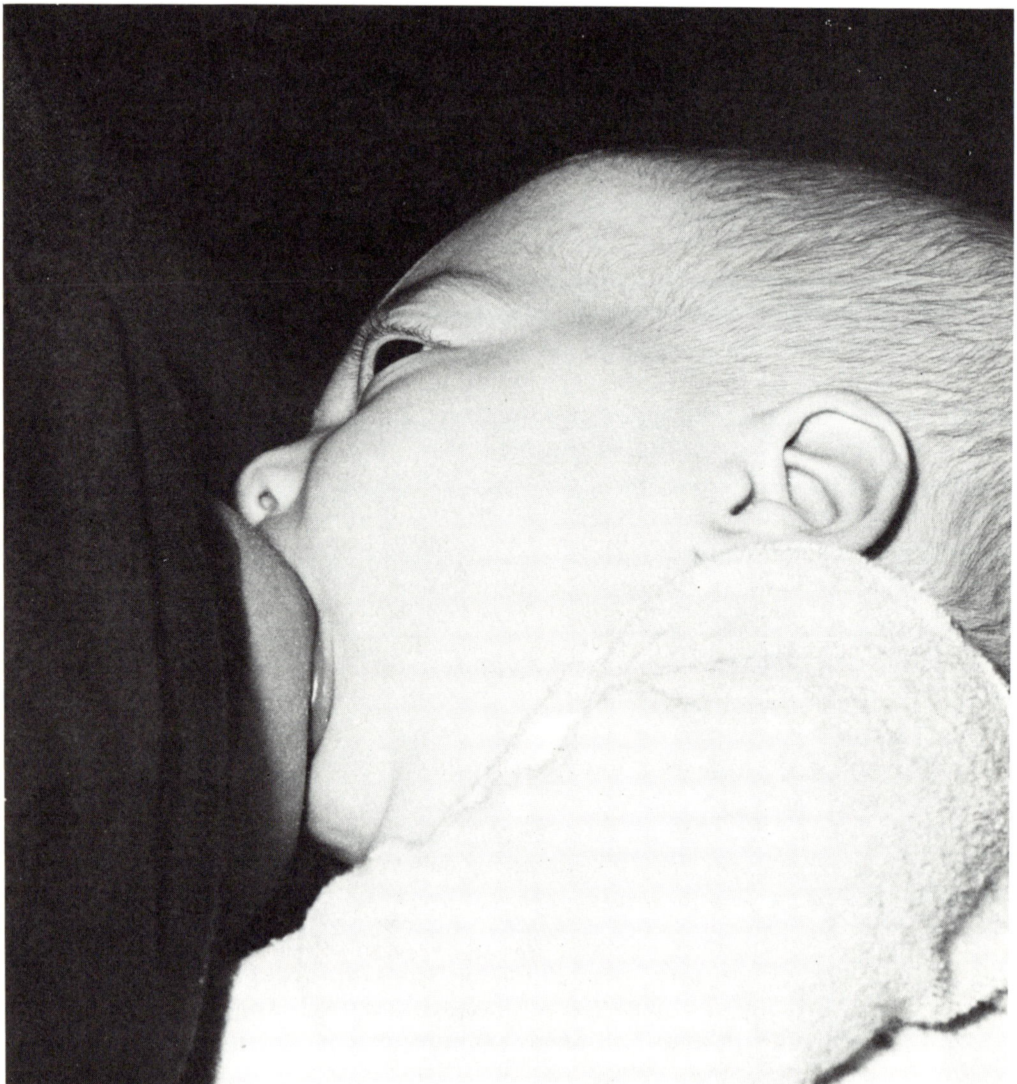

What a champion breastfeeder! Everything is right—mouth open wide, bottom lip curled out, and a loving gaze for Mum. (Photo by Harvey Schwartz)

your doctor, and he or she may prescribe antibiotics. Take these in addition to the three measures mentioned above. Taking antibiotics is not usually a contraindication to breastfeeding, but always mention to your doctor that you are breastfeeding before taking any medication. Breastfeeding is the most helpful thing you can do when you have a breast infection. Feed more often and try not to let the affected side stay full.

The three causes of plugged ducts and breast infections are restrictive clothing, exhaustion and insufficient emptying. A working/breastfeeding mother is more likely to have insufficient emptying and a greater chance of being fatigued, which make her a little more likely to get plugged ducts and breast infections. Try to take a nap with the baby when you come home from work. Also try to nap with your baby on your days off if you need it.

One woman, Mary, a librarian, was definitely able to link exhaustion to her breast infections:

> I was extremely prone to breast infections. It seemed like I had one after another. During the same period my daughter Sara was competing in the nonsleeper Olympics. Eventually I noticed that an especially bad period of being up at night a great deal would be followed by a breast infection. I also started taking large doses of vitamin C and I think that they really made a difference.

Another friend, Geri, a mother of two, also had a series of breast infections:

> I had been breastfeeding Asher without any problems for almost a year and then all of a sudden—*whammo*—I was terribly frustrated by my recurring breast infections. I called a La Leche League Leader about it, and she went over the causes, cures and preventions with me, but I was sure none of them related to me. I finally decided to take her suggestion and go bra-less for a while to see if it would help. Well, I have never had another breast infection, although I am now feeding my second baby. I have gone back to wearing a bra, but I changed styles.

If you suspect a plugged duct and treat it immediately, you should be able to avoid a breast infection. This discussion was not meant to scare you or make you feel that you will be plagued with one plugged duct after another. It is very likely that you will never have even one, but we want you to be knowledgeable about the causes and cures of this problem.

MILK SUPPLY

The problem a working/breastfeeding mother is going to be most concerned about is her milk supply. Just because you are a working/breastfeeding mother does not mean that you will necessarily have a supply problem. And even if you find that you are able to pump fewer ounces, this does not necessarily mean that you will not have a good milk supply during the time you usually feed. For example, mothers who leave only formula for their babies while they work and breastfeed only while they are home usually find that their supply will adjust, although it may take a little time. They will not feel full during the day, but they will be full during the evening and night when they normally breastfeed their babies.

We know of one woman, a magazine editor, who used this method. She told us, "My baby kept up night feeds and my supply stayed good during the hours I was home." Since she never gave the baby a bottle herself, the baby continued to expect only breastfeeds from the mother, and since there was always milk, this pattern was reinforced. This particular little girl continued to breastfeed into toddlerhood.

It is normal for your supply to have ups and downs. If you find you are unable to pump as many ounces at work as you once did, try pumping more often or consider renting an electric pump for a limited period of time. Also try some of the suggestions which follow for a supply problem during your hours at home.

If you feel that you also have less milk when you are breastfeeding your baby, we have several ideas for you. First, make sure you are breastfeeding exclusively during the time you are home. Feed often and for long periods. You can offer to feed the baby—you don't have to wait for him to ask. Don't underestimate the importance of night feeds. They may very well be the key to your success. If you can, take a day off from work and stay in bed breastfeeding your baby all day. Watch your rest and stress level. Don't overdo housekeeping or social efforts. Try to go to bed earlier than usual for the early months of your baby's life.

Look at your diet, too. Your protein intake is very important. At this point in your life, don't try to diet or substitute empty-calorie foods for nutritious ones. You have to feel good to get through this busy period successfully. Keep nutritious snacks in places where you are likely to reach for them. Try to keep nuts and dried fruit in your car, on your desk and in other convenient places. Also keep up your fluid intake.

If none of these suggestions increases your supply adequately, you may want to look into the AXicare Nursing Aid. This device basically consists of a plastic bottle of milk which hangs around your neck. You can use thawed breast milk from your frozen stockpile, but if you are having supply problems, chances are you will use formula in the bottle. A tube comes from the bottle down to your nipple. The baby sucks on your nipple as usual, but gets the supplement in addition to the breast milk. The purpose of this is to provide the baby with an adequate amount of food while your breasts get extra stimulation from the baby, who still associates only breastfeeding with you. The AXicare Nursing Aid is available from Natural Joy and costs around £8 plus p & p.

If continuing the breastfeeding relationship is very important to you, using the AXicare Nursing Aid is preferable to supplementing with a bottle. If your breasts are not full of milk, but the bottle is, you can see how the baby might begin to refuse the breast in favour of the bottle. However, the Nursing Aid will allow you to continue to offer the baby a full supply of milk at your breasts even during the period when you are building up your supply.

The opposite problem—excess milk—can result in leakage. You may suddenly feel your milk let-down or you may simply discover that you are leaking. There is a very simple solution to this problem. You simply need to press your nipples and the milk will stop. An unobtrusive way of doing this is to cross your arms and press them against your nipples. If you are sitting down, you can put your chin in your hand and press into your arm. If leaking is a big problem for you, you can wear nursing pads inside your bra, but always change them as soon as they are wet. You can buy nursing pads in most chemists or make reusable ones from nappies or cotton handkerchiefs.

Remember, any difficulty you have is surmountable. There are many books which deal with the subject of breastfeeding problems at greater length and in greater depth than we have. If you need more help with a problem than your reading has provided, contact your local La Leche League Leader, who is an expert in the area of breastfeeding and will have information which will help you.

6/Mothering

You will undoubtedly get lots of advice about mothering from many sources—your mother, your friends and your doctor. All of these well-meaning people, though, are advising from their own experience, which may or may not apply to you and your family. You'll love, care for and live with this baby for a long, long time, but their interest may be of a much more short-term nature. And although these people may seem to be experts, there is probably no area in your life more worth taking responsibility for than that of mothering.

Once you've chosen to be responsible for your own mothering, the much more difficult task of carrying out your ideas presents itself. Most of us find it very difficult to trust our instincts as parents. Yet that is almost always the best route. Imagine, for instance, that smacking is something you feel you cannot do, but you've just read a book on discipline that clearly states that your child will never respect your authority if she's not smacked. The tendency would be to follow the so-called expert's advice: after all, you have only been a parent a short time. But if, in our imagined instance, you did smack your child, you would most certainly feel guilty and your child would most certainly sense that. Better to follow your instinct and not smack, risk whatever the opposing view suggests will hang over your head (i.e. lack of respect), and have your child see you as an example of honesty and confidence. What a confusing picture you'd paint for your child by acting one way and feeling the opposite in your heart!

Remember that the word "discipline" comes from the word "disciple", and implies nothing about punishment. A disciple is anyone who loves, respects and admires another so much that he patterns his life after that figure. So, in theory, disciplining our children should mean leading a life that they'll want to imitate out of love and respect, not out of fear of punishment. Striving for this lofty ideal is certain to be a monumental task, but one well worth undertaking.

A busy mother doesn't always have time to sit and snuggle when the baby needs it. Putting the baby in a baby carrier is a great way to maximize physical contact, comfort the baby, and still stay on the move when you need to. (Photo by Harvey Schwartz)

SOME BASIC TENETS

Good mothering is good mothering no matter what. But let's face it, there are differences between the family of a working mother and that of a full-time homemaker. Before noting the differences, it's important to have an understanding of the basics of good parenting.

Don't ever underestimate the power of physical contact! A close friend shared this story with us:

> With my first child, I experienced immediate bonding and a close relationship from that point forward. My second, a boy, came before the first was two years old, which greatly increased the skin-to-skin demands made of me. Unfortunately, and unknowingly at first, the baby was the one missing the most, because of his quiet nature. I noticed eventually that I was more short, less patient and loving, with the baby than with the toddler. Having heard of the value of skin contact, I set about consciously increasing it. At every opportunity, I specifically stroked his skin, not even necessarily lovingly. Almost overnight the stroking itself became more loving, and immediately after that my attitude towards this baby changed significantly! Needless to say, loving caresses have become a very special part of our relationship!

Hopefully, of course, physical contact is an integral part of a relationship from the start and is not needed as a remedial measure. Its strength in any loving relationship is a powerful one worth reinforcing. Ashley Montagu, in his book *Touching*, states, "It is the handling, the carrying, the caressing, and the cuddling that we would here emphasize, for it would seem that even in the absence of a great deal else, these are the reassuringly basic experiences the infant must enjoy if it is to survive in some semblance of health."[1]

Another basic tenet of good parenting is focused attention. This, again, is easy to theorize about and difficult to carry out. Dorothy Corkille Briggs, in *Your Child's Self-Esteem*, speaks of focused attention as a "genuine encounter".[2] This is defined vividly in a story by the mother of a pre-school child.

[1]Montagu, *Touching* (Columbia University Press, 1971): 84.
[2]Briggs, *Your Child's Self-Esteem* (Dolphin Books, 1975).
These books are available from LLLGB.

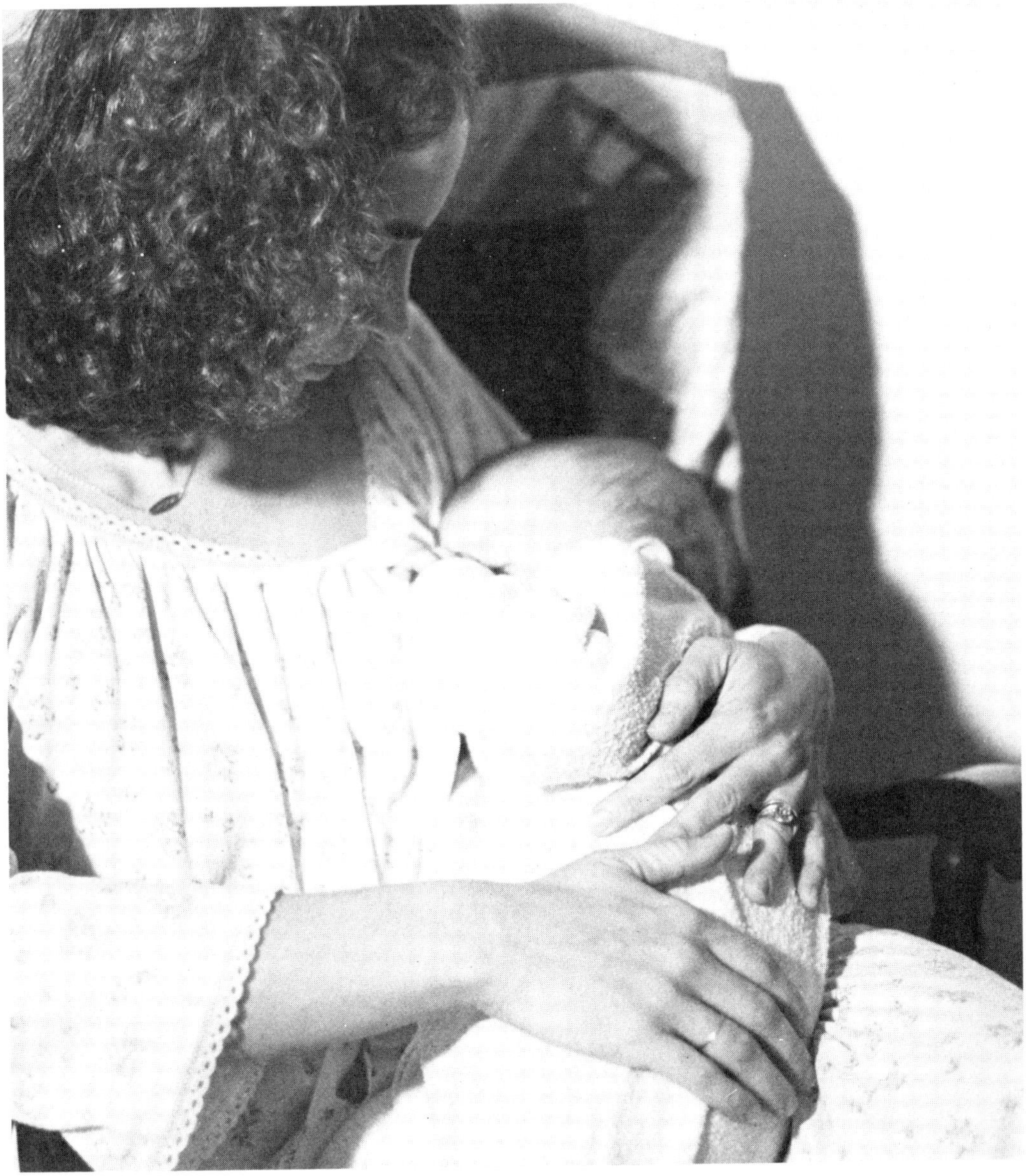

Breastfeeding provides an easy setting for a genuine encounter between a small baby and her mother. (Photo by Harvey Schwartz)

> Katie, at age two, is really pretty independent. But yesterday she was driving me crazy with constant whining and nagging. While trying to finish paying the bills, I had no fewer than fifty interruptions in twenty minutes! Then it occurred to me that at each of her attempts to get attention, I responded with attentive words, but in a vacant tone. So I sat down by her, chatted for a moment, involved myself in her play (peeling the paper off twenty-four new crayons), and concluded the five-minute visit with a hug and a kiss. *Voilà!* Her psyche was so nourished by my expression of her worthiness that she played quietly for the next thirty minutes and I finished my paperwork at last!

This is not to say that focused attention must exist every moment. In Katie's story, five minutes went a long way. Certainly many genuine encounters are best for making a child feel lovable and worthwhile, but at the very least don't let your child feel that you never give your all to her. And don't fall into the common pattern of giving plenty of focused attention in anger or as a response to misbehaviour. Let the majority of time spent in genuine encounter be positive in nature. This effective preventive measure will greatly decrease your child's misbehaviour as she grows. For Katie and her mother, five minutes before the nagging episode would have been even better than the eventual solution.

Development of healthy self-esteem in our children is often seen by new parents as something too abstract for which to strive. Yet self-esteem will undoubtedly play a major part in your child's mental health. *Your Child's Self-Esteem* deals extensively with this subject, and is essential reading for any parent or parent-to-be. The author breaks down her philosophy and does a superb job of bringing her ideas down to earth. Read it to understand the importance of self-image and to learn a practical step-by-step method for improving self-esteem in almost any relationship.

Every baby is different. A rather innocuous statement, right? But when it comes to really allowing for that individuality in our children, many of us do poorly. Something in all of us seems to delight in our child being "just like" her brother, her mother or some textbook image. One of the healthiest things for a parent to experience in this regard is the birth of a second child. When we see the differences in temperament, even at birth, it becomes apparent that each baby is his or her own person.

Your baby's individuality is something to consider as you encounter periods of difficult behaviour. A rather classic case of this was related to us by Gale A.

Although making time for a genuine encounter with two children is a greater challenge, this breastfeeding mother has the opportunity to give attention to her toddler because her baby is content at the breast. (Photo by Harvey Schwartz)

> My first child, Nicholas, was a *very* demanding baby who wanted cuddling and holding around the clock. Yet he went through the "taxing twos" rather quickly and became an absolutely angelic child! His angel spell lasted a long time, from about twenty-seven months to age four and beyond, in spite of a new sister on the scene. Maggie, on the other hand, was a typical "good baby"—feed, play, sleep—for the first ten months of her life. At age eleven months, I swear, she became a "taxing two" and still is today at age three-and-a-half!

There really are some personality traits that your baby "owns". Certainly, your mothering can greatly affect many areas of your child's mental health, but many of her quirks are simply not your domain. The wise parent is the one who is quick to accept this fact and can easily love and nurture a baby for her individuality, not in spite of it.

SPECIFICS FOR WORKING/BREASTFEEDING MOTHERS

Physical contact, focused attention, nurturing self-esteem and an understanding of your child's individuality are all elements of good mothering by both employed and nonemployed mothers. In fact, all of them are important in almost all personal relationships. But the working mother is certainly in a special situation and can greatly enhance her breastfeeding relationship by developing some additional aspects of her mothering skills and style.

Keeping breast milk in adequate supply in spite of limited breastfeeding is the constant concern of a working/breastfeeding mother. No matter how effectively you pump, absolutely nothing can replace time with your baby at your breast! Even though this is certain to be a very busy time in your life, long, leisurely breastfeeds are essential. In addition to keeping up supply, this ensures abundant physical contact, and breastfeeding is the best tranquillizer on the market—for mother and baby alike! Remember that breastfeeding is not only a method of feeding but also provides many other benefits. It is better to allow yourself long periods of time to breastfeed (and nurture, mother and care for) your baby, than it is to merely "feed" the baby with milk from your breasts; keep that in mind to justify the long stretches you spend breastfeeding.

Another aspect of mothering specific to the working woman and her baby is the daily transition from home to work and the childminder's

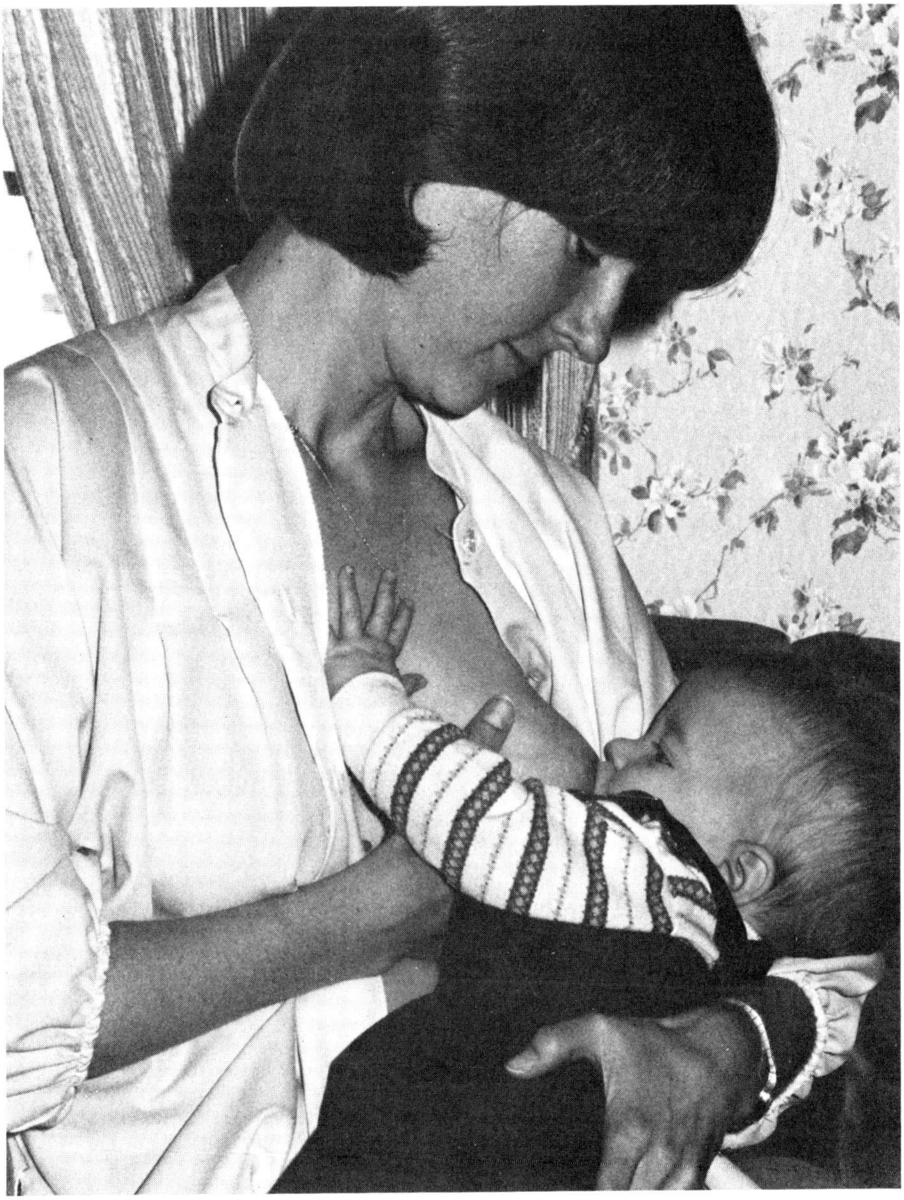

This day starts peacefully for mother and baby and they face the world fuelled for whatever comes their way. (Photo by Harvey Schwartz)

and back home again. Just as we feel that all beginnings are crucial, we feel these transitions are vital, too. They can be relaxed and peaceful or anxious and stress-filled, but planning will certainly alleviate most of the stress. Do make time for one long feed in the morning and then another feed just before you leave home. An insurance clerk in a Denver suburb found that the following routine evolved quite naturally for her.

> Amanda wakes up by five-thirty and we get into my bed together. I don't have to get up until seven, so we cuddle, feed and drowse intermittently for almost two full hours. Then, by the time we get up and into the bath together, we are both fuelled for the day. I try to arrive at the childminder's by eight-twenty, which gives me fifteen minutes to feed once more, settle her in and get out the door. By allowing a fifteen-minute "pad" at the sitter's house, I don't panic if we run a little late leaving home, and I've never been late to work.

Amanda's mother did have a good plan, yet allowed enough time for it to break down a little without causing pandemonium. It also seemed very agreeable to Amanda herself, which was probably an element in its success. If pumping will also be a part of your morning preparation, it will certainly limit your time and add pressure. Streamline your activities and apportion your time carefully. Clearly, although separation anxiety will affect both of you, it will be decreased significantly by a peaceful, confident transition.

The same principles apply to reunions. Loving, relaxed separations and reunions provide a sense of continuity to mother and child, and tense, harassed ones make everybody irritable. So take time for a warm reunion—sit down and feed immediately. Consider doing this at the minder's home if possible, so that you can give your full attention to your baby before you succumb to the necessities of starting supper or reading the mail. Relax and let yourself get back into the "mother" frame of mind.

We've often heard a mother remark, "She's so good for the childminder, but she starts whining the moment I come." And although this may seem to apply more to a toddler or older child, we have also seen it in our babies. A child may nag or become aggressive, whereas a baby will probably cry and be demanding. As taxing as this behaviour may be, it really flatters you as a mother. Your baby cries more at home or in your presence because that is the place she feels it is certain her needs will be met.

It has been said that the best cure for a crying baby is more rest for the mother, but we'll carry that one step further. The best cure for a crying

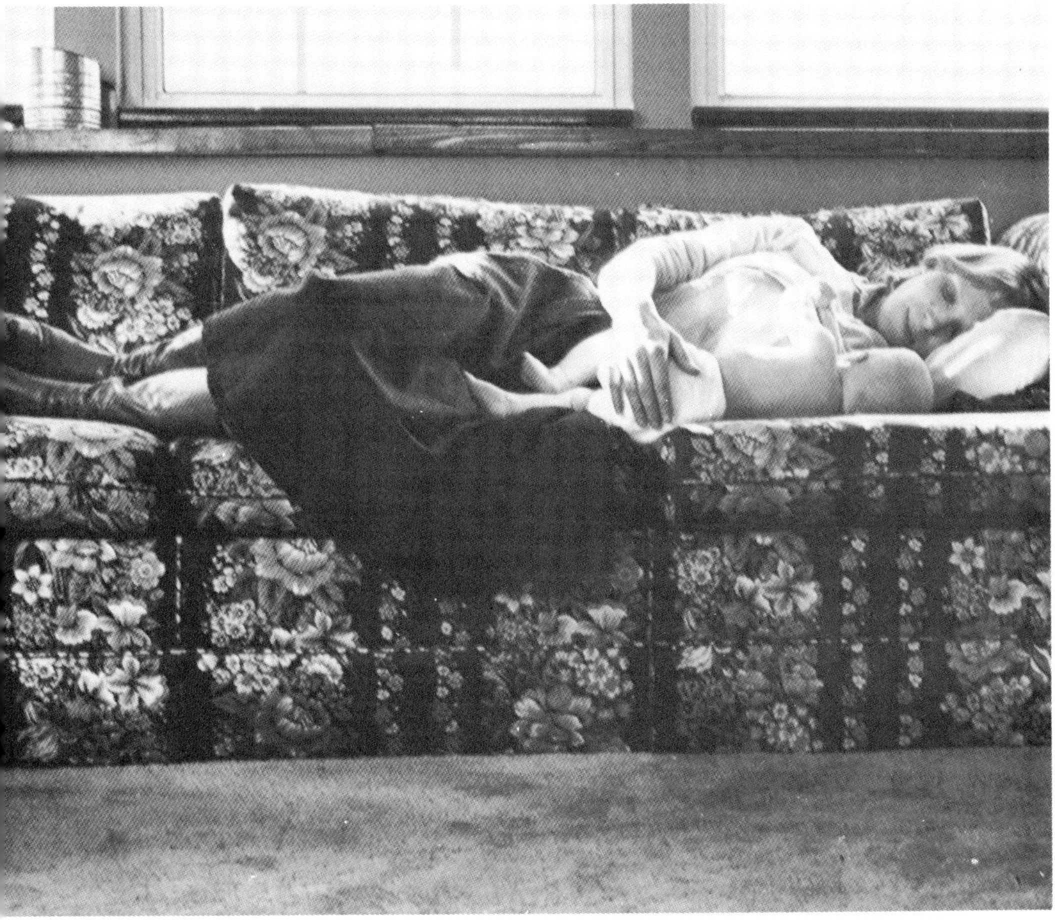

Lying down to feed makes a perfect reunion after a harassing day. It offers rest, physical contact, and moments of tranquillity to the breastfeeding couple. (Photo by Harvey Schwartz)

baby is increased restful contact between mother and baby in the safe haven of home. Usually the only time a working mother can find to have more contact with her baby is at night. Although you will be tired and this idea may not seem worthwhile or appealing to you, many mothers report that it is a very valuable ingredient in meeting the great demands of working while mothering. Many babies simply cannot get enough nurturing from limited daytime contact with their mothers. Experiment. Try keeping her in bed with you or keeping her bed next to yours. Try putting her down for the night in her bed (her room or yours) and then bringing her to your bed for the rest of the night after she wakes for her first night feed. If both you and your partner keep in mind that you are filling her "emotional tank" as much as her stomach, this becomes easier to handle. In fact, we've heard comments from mothers who treasure night feeds because they are so peaceful! In granting a safe haven to your baby, you establish a warm pattern for all your family. You, your partner, your loved ones and your children will all learn that home is a place to unwind and feel at ease.

Now that we've presented an idealized image of mothering for you, let's step back and face reality for a bit. The word "ideal" means the *aim* of endeavour, something not real or practical. Aim for great heights, but know that the reality will often not be as lofty. So don't be too hard on yourself—you can't be a supermum. Remain flexible and let your priorities change for your new "mother lifestyle". By all means, don't expect things to get back to normal. That "normal" is history now, just as your single life was gone forever when you married. And as when you married, your life has undergone a permanent change that is hard to adjust to, but now there are more rewards than you thought possible!

Seek support if you need it, in any appropriate form. Maybe your partner will provide all you need, or maybe you can refuel by phoning a supportive friend. If structured support sounds good, try La Leche League, although since it is not geared to the working woman, you may or may not feel supported. But often a woman who is secure in what she is doing finds she can accept the encouragement she needs and discard any nonsupportive comments. If La Leche League is not the answer for you, search for or create a support group specifically for working/breastfeeding mothers or parents.

The prime ingredients to good mothering are long, loving, physical contact, plenty of focused attention, careful attention to development of self-esteem and an understanding acceptance of your child's individuality. However, as a working mother you will be compelled to give consideration to a few other areas. Find ways to provide extra physical contact in a limited time frame; plan and execute beginnings and reunions with a minimum of stress; establish the time at the breast as a loving, happy time, so that it is always preferred over a mere feed from a bottle. Make your home a warm, safe haven, with an atmosphere of loving acceptance for you and your family. And after all that, *give yourself a break!*

7/Alternatives

A GREAT WAY to think about some alternatives is to see how another culture views the issue of working and breastfeeding. Israel is a country where almost every mother is a working mother. Although breastfeeding is not as prevalent as it is, for example, in the United States, there is official encouragement to breastfeed. An Israeli La Leche League Leader, Toby Gish, shared the following information with us about working/breastfeeding mothers in Israel.

> Israeli women have a three-month paid maternity leave and when they return to work, they can work an hour less each day for the same pay if they are breastfeeding.
>
> More and more Israeli women are electing to continue to breastfeed when they return to work for several reasons. First is their reluctance to leave the breastfeeding experience. Second, it's some emotional compensation for leaving the baby. Third, there is increased public awareness of the importance of breastfeeding due to La Leche League, newspaper articles, etc. Fourth is the availability and popularity of the Kaneson Expressing and Feeding Bottle for a reasonable price.
>
> Most women are absent for only one or two feeds. There are those who elect to pump and leave a bottle of mother's milk for the *metapelet* (childminder) to give the baby. Some choose to replace one meal for older babies with a fruit meal and others leave a bottle of formula.
>
> Some women are finding other solutions. Lisa has received permission from the manager of the bank where she works to have her daughter brought to her for a breastfeeding break instead of a coffee break. Her manager even offered her the use of his office. Ruthi took Elisheva back to the university with her. Donna Ron, our kibbutznik La Leche League Leader, kept the kibbutz switchboard running for seven months with her son happily stretched out on a blanket next to her. The best endorsement for the magic of a happy breastfeeding experience here are these mothers who are finding ingenious ways to stretch their maternity leaves.

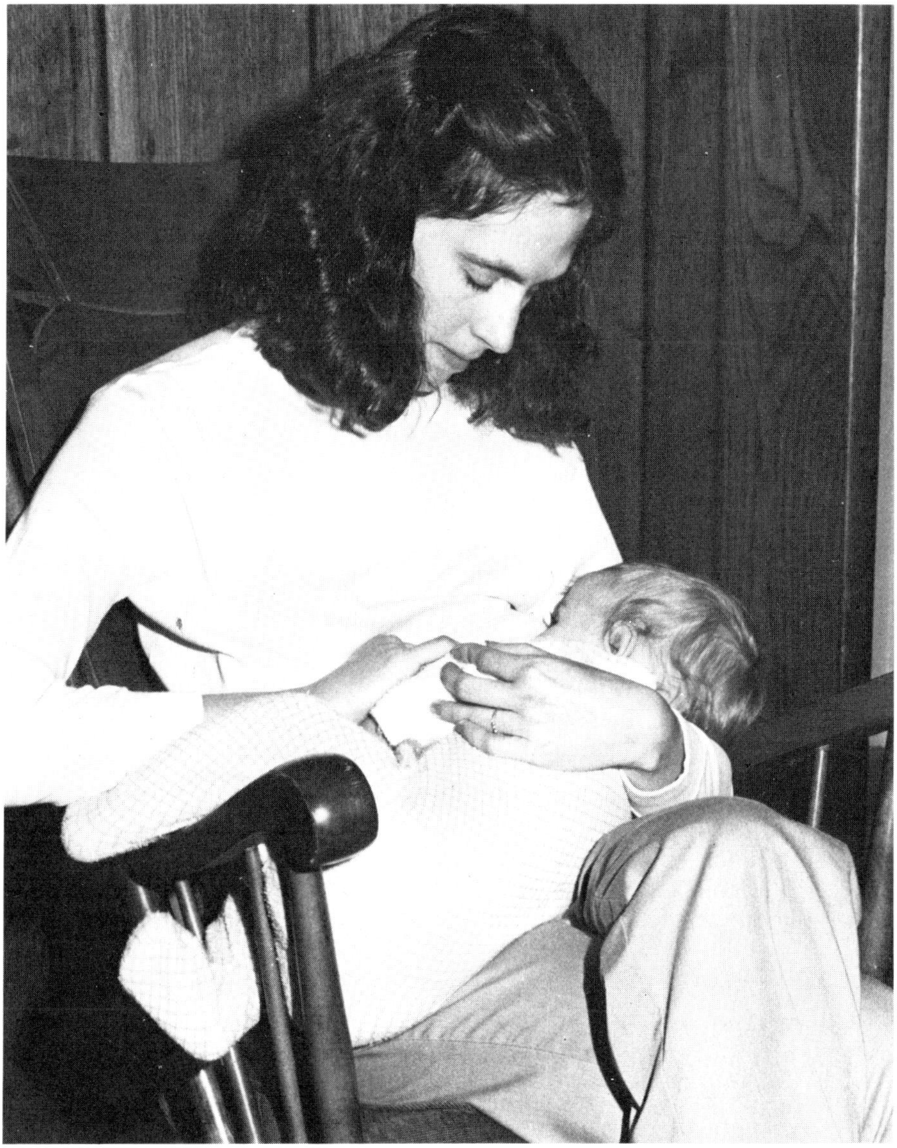

Mum's lunch break can be a breastfeeding break too, whether at the minder's, at home, or at work. The useful knack of breastfeeding discreetly (by pulling up your blouse from below) is easily mastered. (Photo by Harvey Schwartz)

We have also seen some creative approaches to managing working and breastfeeding in our culture which do not involve working a forty-hour week and leaving the baby in someone else's care for the entire time. We would like to share alternatives some have found. Perhaps you will find one which will be relevant to your situation and appealing to you. Or perhaps the following ideas and flexible solutions will encourage you to come up with one of your own, best suited to your lifestyle.

BREASTFEEDING AT LUNCH

Many women who are strongly against an eight- to nine-hour separation from their babies come up with a way to breastfeed during the working day. In order to do this, they must have flexibility of worktime or workplace. Terry S., who works in a bank, told us:

> I made an arrangement with my supervisor that allowed me to combine my two fifteen-minute breaks with my half-hour lunch break, so I could take an hour at lunchtime. This gave me time to drive to my childminder's house. Fortunately, I was able to find a minder who lived close to work and who didn't mind my daily visit. I fed Jeremy from about eight-thirty until eight forty-five at the childminder's before I left, then I breastfed him again at about twelve-fifteen and spent the rest of our time together holding, cuddling, rocking and playing with him, or whatever he seemed to want.
>
> This was necessary for me. I simply could not bear that much time away from my baby. I have heard other women say that two separations in one day makes it harder for them or for the baby, but it didn't work that way for us. My baby greatly enjoyed our time together, and it relieved my guilt feelings somewhat. Jeremy usually took a nap after I left and then took a bottle about three or four and breastfed again eagerly shortly after six when I returned. If it hadn't been for this arrangement with my understanding and cooperative childminder, I don't know what I would have done!

Going to the baby during lunchtime is an alternative many women have used happily. We know of a woman who, when she was a psychiatric nurse, lived very close to the hospital at which she worked. Because of this proximity, she employed a childminder to come to her home. She managed to come home often enough to breastfeed her baby at every feed and never had to leave any bottles at all.

Another possibility, which calls for a sympathetic employer and an extremely sympathetic childminder, is to have her bring the baby to you

When you consider the option of taking your baby to work, don't rule anything out. Many jobs offer surprising possibilities, so think creatively. (Photo by Harvey Schwartz)

at work when he is ready to feed. Many celebrities use a variation of that theme: they hire a minder to come to work with the baby. This allows them great flexibility for breastfeeding or for play and/or care. Many well-known personalities, such as Lynn Redgrave, Goldie Hawn and Esther Rantzen made extra efforts to breastfeed their babies. The 22 February, 1982, issue of *Time* magazine stated: "Although she [actress Jaclyn Smith] has not yet chosen a project, she is adamant about breastfeeding on the set. 'I'll convert my trailer into a nursery,' she says. It may complicate her life, but Smith believes the enrichment outweighs the disadvantages."

In the USA there was a lot of publicity about Linda Eaton, the firefighter from Iowa, because she arranged to have her son, Ian, brought to her at work for breastfeeding. This publicity occurred in January 1979 when Ian was three months old. She only breastfed him in her personal time, during a period when her co-workers also received visits from their families. She was sacked over this issue, and she took her case before the Civil Rights Commission.

The September 1980 issue of *Ms.* magazine reported that the Civil Rights Commission "found the city's action to be based upon 'opposition to the physical act of breastfeeding' and ruled that 'singling out an employee for different treatment because of the employee's breastfeeding is discriminating on the basis of sex.' " The Commission awarded her $2,000 for emotional stress, $145 for back pay and $26,442 in lawyer's fees. Linda Eaton found it necessary to resign two weeks after this ruling, however, because of harassment from her fellow firefighters.

Although most of us will not meet the extreme opposition which Linda Eaton faced, we cannot usually afford the luxury of having a nanny at work with us either. But even the practical application of this option, going to your baby during lunchtime, has its drawbacks as well as advantages. Inconvenience is clearly the major disadvantage here, either in the form of extra travel to and from the baby, or the necessity of making special arrangements in your timetable. Your working day may actually be lengthened so that you can have an adequate break and/or lunchtime to travel and breastfeed.

The most obvious advantage of arranging to breastfeed your baby during your working day is that you can probably avoid the inconvenience of pumping at work. But it is also a real plus for the baby, for he receives the extra physical and emotional contact with his mother. And the fact that you are breastfeeding instead of pumping will definitely help you maintain your milk supply more easily. Although pumping can be effective, there is really no substitute for having your baby at your breast.

So evaluate this alternative in terms of your own preferences and priorities and the needs and personality of your baby. We recommend this plan to the woman who is highly opposed to pumping at work, yet clearly wishes her baby to have breast only, and whose childminder is conveniently located. It may also be a solution for the woman whose baby refuses a bottle. However, this is not the best choice for a woman with sporadic lunchtimes and breaks, or when the bother of arrangements with work and minder cause more tension than they are worth.

PART-TIME WORK

When a working woman becomes a mother, there are several options open to her. She can stay at home full time, she can return to work full time, or she can make a compromise between these two parts of her life and return to work part time. Happily, part-time work can be temporarily or permanently combined with motherhood. If you do decide to choose this option you will undoubtedly have an easier time continuing to breastfeed than if you were working full time. You can take the advice and information this book contains about breastfeeding while working full time and cut it back to fit your own needs. Depending on how many hours you work each day, you may not have to pump at all.

Dottie Lamm, a popular American columnist for the *Denver Post* and First Lady of the state of Colorado, told us of her part-time work arrangement when she was breastfeeding her son Scott:

> I had a part-time job which was generally thirteen and a half hours a week, but sometimes it was extended to twenty. Either way, I was able to miss only one feed each day I worked, and I only worked three days a week. At the age of six weeks, I began to get Scott used to a substitute formula-feeding for the times I would be gone. He didn't like it the first time, but the second time he gobbled it up eagerly. So I felt very relieved and free to go back to work at seven weeks, as I had planned. I never used a breast pump because I only missed one feed and didn't find it necessary. Also, I felt it was very good for him to have adapted to both breast and bottle milk, so occasionally on non-working days my husband and I could go out in the evening and have a babysitter to give him a substitute bottle. However, during the time I was breastfeeding and working, we did not go out very much, because I felt very strongly that the breastfeeding should predominate.

Another successful example is Sharmon Z. She continued to teach three afternoons a week for three hours each day after her baby was born. She fed Emily when she dropped her off at her mother-in-law's house and then again as soon as she returned from work. Using this arrangement, she never had to pump a single bottle.

An interesting idea that also falls into the category of part-time work is that of job sharing. It seems to be an economic fact that part-time work pays less per hour than full-time work, regardless of training or position. That is the problem which job sharing solves. Two women, perhaps both mothers of young children, can split in half a job that is usually held by one person. They can do this either by dividing the day in half or by working two and a half days per week. Two teachers in Denver split a teaching job in half by choosing to take six-week turns. This arrangement would not be very helpful to a breastfeeding mother but they could have arranged to split the day in half if that would have suited their needs better.

This type of job splitting is a fairly new idea and has not been implemented extensively. Although it may not be feasible for some jobs, it can easily be done in many trades, most clerical positions, and in some professions. Even if it hasn't been done at your place of work before, and especially if you know of someone who would be interested in splitting your job with you, why not approach your management people and discuss it?

Some women will have the option of simply reducing their hours. If you are in some type of professional private practice, you may be able to adjust your schedule to your new demands by taking fewer clients.

Perhaps you can ask your employer to give you fewer hours. We know of two social workers who did this. One of them, Patty, told us how she did it. "After Ricky was born I took a couple of months off from work. Instead of going back to forty hours a week I asked for only twenty hours a week. As Ricky got a little older and started taking more solids by about nine months I didn't need to leave as much breast milk for him. At that point I went up to thirty hours a week." Ricky is now two years old and Patty has not increased her hours again because she feels that this is the maximum amount she can handle along with the demands of motherhood.

Part-time employment combined with some of the other alternatives suggested in this chapter may work well for you, too. In the beginning you may be able to work while keeping the baby with you, and later you may need to use a childminder, depending on your type of work. However, you will be the one to decide on the time and amount of daycare.

There are some variations on the part-time work theme. If you want to work much less than full-time but to keep one foot in the working world, examine your skills and see if they can be restructured a little. For example, can you take the work you've been doing in the office for someone else and do it at home for yourself? We know of a landscape architect and a woman who does public relations and editing who have both done this very successfully. Along these same lines, some women (and men, too) bring home some of their work to cut down on out-of-home hours. People whose work involves a computer or a typewriter can usually do this without too much trouble.

Sometimes you can take a skill like teaching and do it on a freelance basis. Anne Price, a co-author of this book, was a secondary school teacher before her children were born. Since then she has done various types of part-time teaching. She has taught speed reading, various courses, and has also done supply teaching. Some nurses are now choosing to do medicals for insurance companies at their own convenience rather than working in more traditional jobs. There are probably many other professions which will lend themselves to this "a little bit here and a little bit there" type of work.

Like any alternative, part-time work has its pros and cons. The main disadvantage is that you will earn less money than if you had a full work schedule. (But you will also be spending less on childcare.) It is possible that reducing your job to part time will mean missing promotions or pay rises. And, depending on your particular job, reducing your hours may or may not be practical.

However, the advantage of extra time could be very special for both you and your baby, and could perhaps help to alleviate feelings of guilt and anxiety you may have. Naturally you will need to do less pumping, or perhaps none at all. Since you will be nursing more your milk supply will be more easily maintained. But the most important advantage is, of course, the time you will have for increased contact with your baby.

TAKING BABY TO WORK

A third alternative is to bring your baby to work. This option is not feasible for many women, but for those with a sufficiently flexible work situation, it can be very worthwhile. It works best with a tiny baby who sleeps more and needs less entertainment. Also, leaving the baby during the early months may cause the mother the most anxiety. Depending on your type of work, however, you may be able to keep bringing your baby in with you indefinitely.

We have spoken to many women who have taken their babies to work, both successfully and unsuccessfully. Usually the first thing that comes to the employer's mind is the possibility that the time you spend caring for your baby will end up costing him or her money. One solution to this dilemma is suggested in Diana Korte's article in *Colorado Woman* magazine, "Baby on the Job".[1] She refers to a mother of four, Pat Uhlir, who works in a bakery. Pat simply charged her employer a flat fee for her work. That way breastfeeding her baby on the job was not a disadvantage to her employer. She just stayed at work until she was finished. Ms Korte reported that other women who have taken their babies to work keep track of their "baby time" and add that amount back to the time they spend on the job.

Nancy Bamford, a co-author of this book, tried taking her two boys, then aged nine months and two years, to a part-time book-keeping job. Although she had her employer's blessing, she found it difficult to accomplish her work with the boys there. Their ages and the fact that there were two children involved certainly contributed to the difficulty of the situation. Nancy comments:

> But mostly it was too hard for me emotionally. I was paid by the hour for working hours, and could really feel free to take as many baby hours as I cared to spend. But I always ended up feeling that I was cheating my boss by playing with the boys or that I was cheating the children by doing my job. Although the situation was ideal, the arrangement, for me, was mentally unfeasible. (P.S.: The employer's wife now takes their baby with her and does the book-keeping.)

Another woman who held a high-ranking position in a community centre found that she had no trouble bringing her infant daughter to work. She kept a carry cot in her office and was easily able to breastfeed without interruption in the privacy of her office.

The September 1980 issue of *Ms.* magazine reports on the case of Barbara Koser of Eugene, Oregon, an administrative clerk for the Census Bureau. She began bringing her son Jefferson to work when he was one week old. She had no difficulty caring for the baby at work or managing her duties on the job, but shortly after she began this practice, the acting manager sent her a memo saying that she could no longer bring her baby to work. The reason cited was that the baby was not covered by the firm's insurance liability and the Bureau didn't want to

[1]Korte, "Baby on the Job", *Colorado Woman* (April/May 1979): 8.

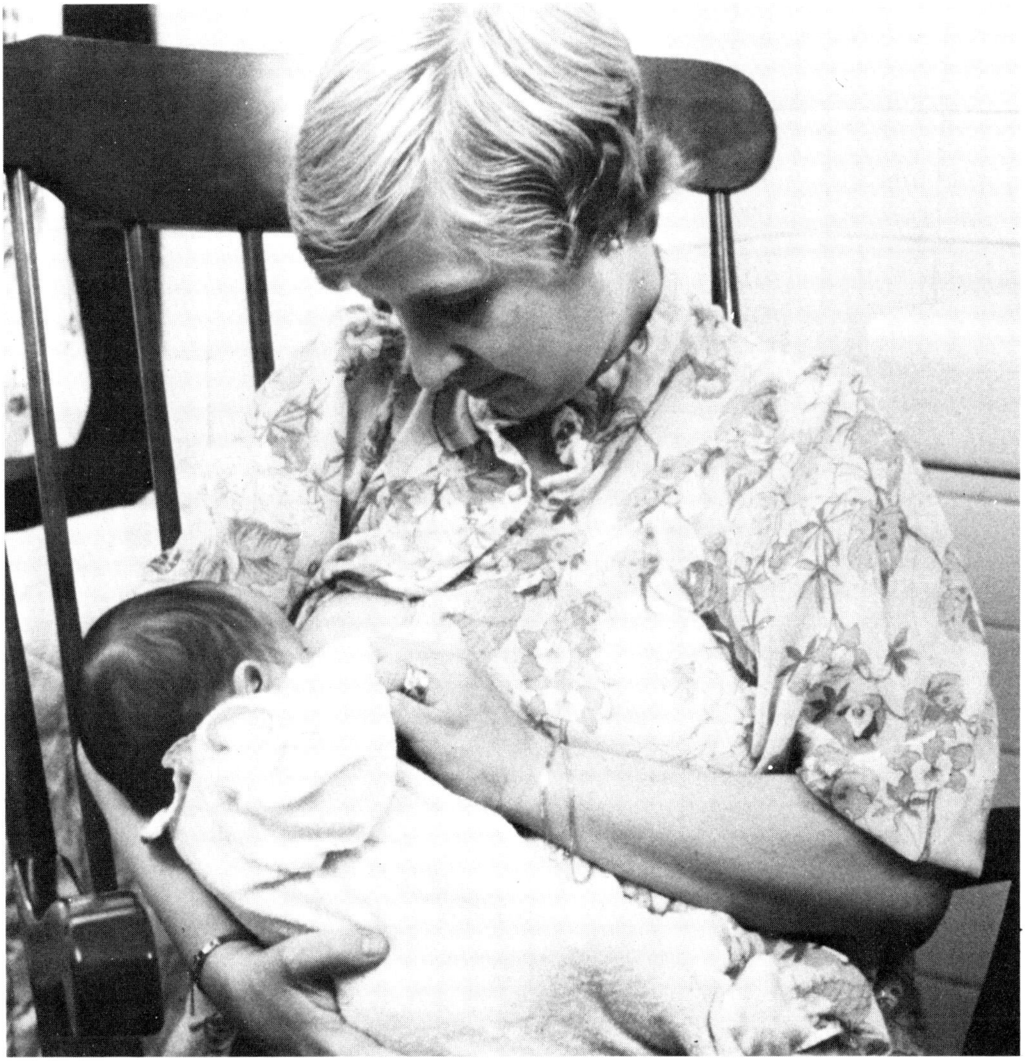

If your baby is brought to you at work on a regular basis, you'll both be happier if you set up a comfortable spot for these feeds. (Photo by the University of Colorado Health Science Center)

be open to a possible legal action.

Ms Koser took a very creative approach to this problem. She went to Northwest Legal Advocates, a non-profitmaking public-interest legal practice in Eugene, with her case. They helped her to draft a document which exempted the Bureau from liability should her son be injured at work. The Bureau accepted this document and Jefferson was back at work with his mother two weeks later.

Of course, having a profession which offers the possibility of self-determined hours and a private office is a big help if you want to bring your baby to work. Similarly, being self-employed or high up in management also eliminates the ticklish question of securing your employer's permission.

Although many women take babies to work very successfully, it would be unfair if we did not mention that it is undoubtedly difficult to satisfy both the baby's needs and the demands of a job in one time slot. For many mothers it could certainly be compared to doing two full-time jobs simultaneously. However, this arrangement remains attractive to some women because they feel strongly that they should not be separated from their babies. As Pat Uhlir of Colorado, said, "I don't want to miss a moment of my baby's life. If I'm going to have babies, I don't have to leave them just because I have to work."

Another advantage is the elimination of costly childcare fees and thus the ability to take home more earnings. Needless to say a mother who takes her baby to work has also eliminated the worry about pumping or storing her milk or milk supply problems.

OTHER OPTIONS

Yet another innovative idea is the establishment of a crèche on the work premises. This should become a growing trend as women realize it is beneficial to have their children near them and are less afraid to assert themselves for legitimate needs. Employers will also realize that a crèche on the premises will help attract and keep employees. Obviously it takes a large work force to justify setting up a crèche, such as is found in a factory, hospital or large institution.

For businesses which don't have enough employees to justify a crèche, there exists the possibility of pooling with several nearby places of employment. For example, several office buildings or hospital buildings near each other could organize a joint crèche. If such a crèche were to be run on a non-profitmaking basis, the parents would benefit from the lower fee. Or perhaps more money could be applied to crèche

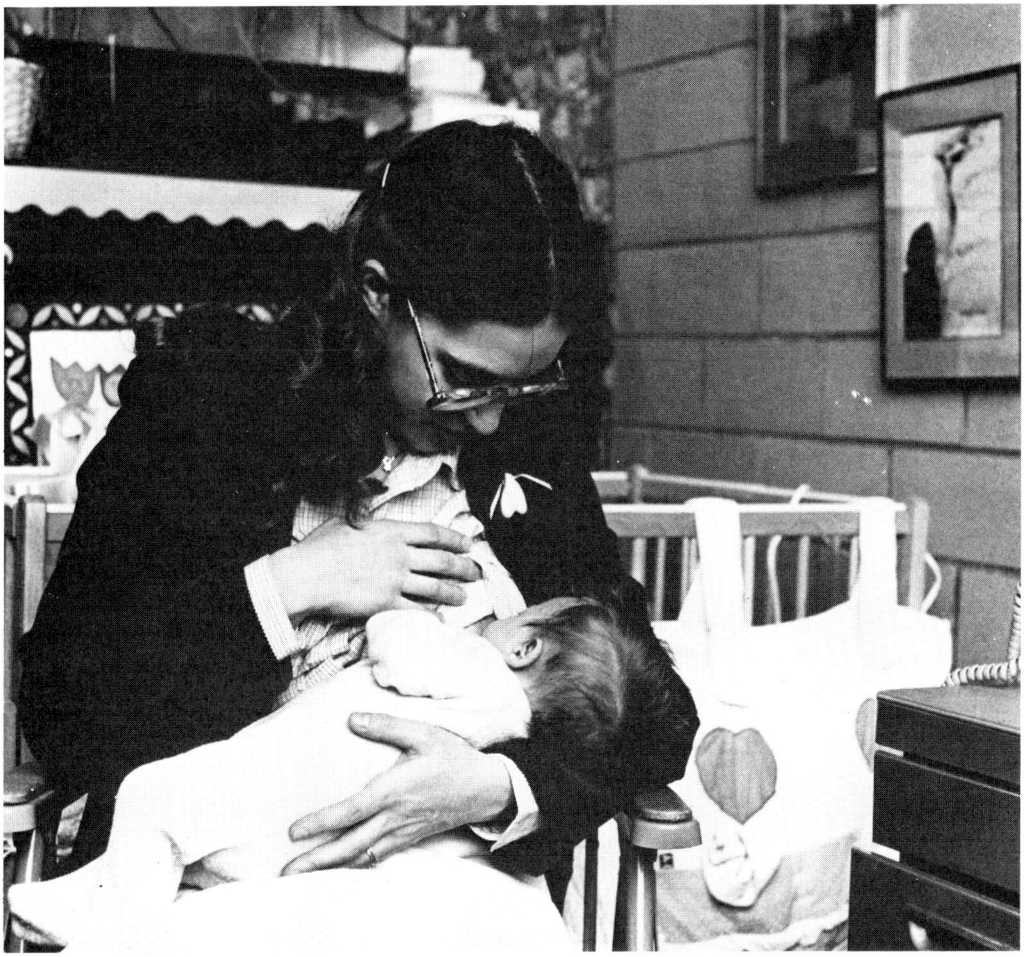

A tiny baby may fit easily into mother's working day. (Photo by Anne Price)

workers' salaries and a better staff could be hired. Because of its proximity, mothers could easily go to their babies and children (for breastfeeding or just for contact) at breaks and lunchtime if desired.

A book called *Who Cares for Children? A Survey of Child Care Services in North Carolina*, compiled by the Learning Institute of North Carolina, reports on this subject:

> Some companies and unions have set up crèches for their own workers. Generally parents pay for this service on a sliding scale, and the company covers the rest. The Skyland Textile Company in Morgantown, North Carolina; KLH, which manufactures stereophonograph systems and other high fidelity equipment in Cambridge, Massachusetts; and the Amalgamated Clothing Workers in Chicago have all set up crèches for their workers' children—and sometimes for the children of other people in the community. It has been found that the establishment of such facilities cuts down absenteeism and generally improves the morale of women workers who are confident that their children are being well cared for.
>
> Nearly one hundred hospitals have set up crèches (some running for twenty-four hours) for the children of nurses and other employees. Some universities provide facilities for the children of their students and faculty—and women's groups are pressing more universities to do the same.[2]

If your place of work doesn't have a crèche at present, and you would like to see one begun, look into organizing one yourself. Are there enough children to make it worthwhile? Find out if there is interest among your co-workers. How supportive would the management be? Would it be possible to combine with other offices in the area? Explore the possibilities and see how far you can go towards creating the best care situation for you and your children.

Don't be afraid to approach management to pursue your needs. You may need a private place to pump; you may want your company to consider buying an electric breast pump; you may be trying to set up a crèche. Whatever you need, go ahead and ask—your needs and the needs of your baby are important. Be flexible, creative and assertive and make the best decisions for you!

[2]Learning Institute of North Carolina, *Who Cares for Children? A Survey of Child Care Services* (1974).

Afterword

THE FIRST RESPONSE from most women, when asked about their experiences while working and breastfeeding, is usually a comment about feeling apart from the rest of the world. These women find very quickly that their friends fall neatly into two very separate categories. Some are earth mothers. Some are career women. None are both. Earth mothers breastfeed, eat brown rice and talk of long, blissful hours with their children. They assure you that breastfeeding is the *only* way to feed your baby and can't understand *why* you would go back to work. Career women talk at great length of "quality time" and assure you that children left with minders grow up to be more independent and just can't see *why* you bother to breastfeed.

Somehow almost everyone a mother (or mother-to-be) meets finds an opportunity to attack at least some of that mother's choices. Rather than gaining support from the two factions, often a working mother who breastfeeds finds that her earth mother friends criticize her working and her career women friends don't understand her breastfeeding. Of course, these women are not at fault for this split in society; society itself is to blame.

Nor is the rift a product of the twentieth-century; instead, this dichotomy has been developing throughout history. In an agricultural society, the woman was usually at home, running the home. Her "work" was child-rearing, cooking, cleaning and sewing. She also did many tasks considered "men's work", like maintaining a *large* garden and splitting the mountains of firewood required, because those things were done close to the home. The men primarily did the work that had to be done away from home, such as hunting, farming a crop for barter, fishing and felling and hauling logs for firewood.

As the industrial age evolved women remained at home and men remained away from home, now at work in a shop or factory. The demarcation was again along sexual lines. In fact sexism probably became more pronounced because men often laboured twelve to fourteen hours a day, seven days a week. That meant that women were likely to take on chores that men may have done before, like home maintenance, tending the animals and the like. The gap then widened, with women coming to "own" all family- and home-related work and men being sole "owners" of the task of breadwinning. This was the beginning of the split between work ethics and humanitarian ethics.

Imagine an early industrial age father. The emphasis in his world was on producing more products faster. He was valued for the end goal (the product) and not for his inherent human worth. Understandably he became goal-oriented very quickly. The mother, however, was in an environment in which there were no products. Each day meant more baby care, more meals and more firewood. There is certainly little in running a household that amounts to a final product! Had she not gained fulfilment from the process itself she might have gone insane! Just as men easily became goal-oriented, women quite naturally were process-oriented. These outlooks, obviously, were inherent in the roles, not in gender.

The gap began to narrow during World War I when women did "men's work" in factories because the men were at war. Slowly, since that time, women are coming to be seen as a viable part of the work force. Men are now being freed to take on more tasks at home as well. Interestingly, even as the division of roles according to sex seems to be narrowing, the basic division between the world of work, with its own ethics, and the home, with its quite different ethics, seems almost as universal as ever. For instance, it's "bad" for home values to get in the way at work. Management is often wary of the employee who turns down a promotion for a human value, like the desire for some time with his or her family. Look, too, at the differences between the ways we dress, talk and behave at work and at home. You will probably find them quite marked!

Today there are many women who continue to breastfeed after they return to work. They are trying to combine the worlds of work and the home by carrying some of their mothering duties with them to work. They must deal with the issue of pumping milk for their babies and, in some cases, even bring their babies to work. Their pioneer efforts are definitely of value for all of society and constitute the first step in changing society's outlook.

In this book we have discussed many women who have managed to blend these roles. In the recent past this was rarely done—rarely even considered. One of the reasons, we feel, was not that it was impossible or impractical, but because there were emotional constraints which prevented women from feeling validation for their mothering side after stepping through the office door. There was a feeling that anything in the home/mothering realm had to be dropped off at the childminder's, and it was just not thought possible that one might continue mothering (even mentally) while working. Generally, it is not the difficulties of pumping and storing breast milk that have prevented women from continuing to breastfeed after they return to work. Instead, it has been, for the most part, the difficulty of mentally combining the two roles at one time and place. However, we feel that it is possible to bring together these two roles, and we have tried in this book to present practical ideas for doing so.

Booklist

Most of the books listed below are easily obtainable at bookshops; books marked with an asterisk can only be obtained through the La Leche League at present. All the books and the leaflets listed can be ordered from LLLGB. Write for an order form to: LLLGB, BM 3424, London WC1V 6XX. Tel 01 404 5011

The Womanly Art of Breastfeeding, LLL Manual.
Breast is Best, Drs P. & A. Stanway, Pan Books.
The Experience of Breastfeeding, Sheila Kitzinger, Penguin.

How to Really Love Your Child, Dr R. Campbell, Victor Books.
**The Family Bed: An Age Old Concept in Child Rearing*, Tine Thevenin.
Your Child's Self Esteem, D. C. Briggs, Dolphin Books.
Touching, Ashley Montagu, Harper & Row.

New Life, A. & J. Balaskas, Sidgwick & Jackson.
Pregnancy and Childbirth, Sheila Kitzinger, Michael Joseph.
Birth at Home, Sheila Kitzinger, Oxford University Press.
**Caesarian Birth*, The Caesarian Support Group of Cambridge. (Their current address is obtainable from LLLGB.)

LA LECHE LEAGUE LEAFLETS

11 *Managing Nipple Problems*
29 *Sore Breast* (plugged ducts and infections)
80 *Breastfeeding After a Caesarean Birth*
167 *The Biological Specificity of Milk* (why to feed a baby breast rather than other milk)
715 *Crying—Why and What to Do*

Useful Addresses

La Leche League of Great Britain
BM 3424
London WC1V 6XX
Tel. 01 404 5011

National Childbirth Trust
9 Queensborough Terrace
Bayswater
London W2 3TB

Cannon Babysafe
Ashley Road
Tottenham
London N17 9LH

Egnell-Ameda Ltd
Quarry House
Mill Lane
Uckfield
East Sussex

Natural Joy (AXicare pumps and accessories)
1 Howard Close
London N11 1EH
Tel. 01 368 1077 (Twenty-four hours)

Robbins Medical Supplies Ltd
Otterburn
22 The Avenue
Hitchin
Hertfordshire SG4 9RL

Index